What people are saying about …

YOU CAN STILL WEAR CUTE SHOES

"Lisa made me laugh and clearly is making the most of her life as a pastor's wife. She constantly points us to the Savior as the only one who can make sense of this hectic life. This book should be required reading for pastors' wives around the world."

Kathy MacDonald, wife of Pastor James
MacDonald, Harvest Bible Chapel

"Every pastor's wife can benefit from reading this book! I desperately wish I'd had something like this to guide my steps when I first became a PW! Witty, insightful, and authentic, this book is entertaining and profoundly helpful for women trying to navigate the choppy waters of ministry, marriage, and family. Lisa writes about her own experiences in an engaging and transparent way, providing a sense of connectedness and community for her fellow pastors' wives. I highly recommend this book to any woman who finds herself *married to the ministry!*"

Jodie Howerton, wife of Pastor Mike
Howerton, Overlake Christian Church

"It is difficult to find real, relevant resources for pastor's wives. But Lisa has really delivered. This book will be an encouragement for any woman in leadership."

Lori Wilhite, wife of Pastor Jud
Wilhite, Central Christian Church

"In *You Can Still Wear Cute Shoes,* Lisa McKay is a steady hand at the elbow of every newly minted pastor's wife. With candid vigor and gentle humor, she helps pastors' wives understand how to walk in grace—without losing their style. What's more, she offers access to a real-time community of pastors' wives who assemble online in order to support and care for one another and, if needed, talk each other off the ledge. Are you a pastor's wife? Take a deep breath, strap on your sassy sandals, and dig in to this book."

Bonnie Grove, author of *Your Best
You and Talking to the Dead* and wife
of Pastor Steve Grove, Louise Street
Community Church of the Nazarene

"Finally a book that's honest, relevant, and a fresh voice for pastor's wives. Lisa McKay's writing style makes you feel like you are sitting down to have a cup of coffee with a girlfriend. And ministry wives definitely need a good girlfriend! If you are looking for a special gift for your pastor's wife, you've found it. And if you are a pastor's wife, you need this book!"

Jill Savage, author of *Real Moms … Real Jesus,*
CEO of Hearts at Home, and wife of Pastor
Mark Savage, Crosswinds Community Church

You Can Still Wear Cute Shoes

You Can Still Wear Cute Shoes

AND OTHER GREAT ADVICE FROM
AN UNLIKELY PREACHER'S WIFE

LISA MCKAY

David C Cook
transforming lives together

YOU CAN STILL WEAR CUTE SHOES
Published by David C. Cook
4050 Lee Vance View
Colorado Springs, CO 80918 U.S.A.

David C. Cook Distribution Canada
55 Woodslee Avenue, Paris, Ontario, Canada N3L 3E5

David C. Cook U.K., Kingsway Communications
Eastbourne, East Sussex BN23 6NT, England

David C. Cook and the graphic circle C logo
are registered trademarks of Cook Communications Ministries.

The Web site addresses recommended throughout this book are offered as a
resource to you. These Web sites are not intended in any way to be or imply an
endorsement on the part of David C. Cook, nor do we vouch for their content.

All Scripture quotations, unless otherwise noted, are taken from the *Holy Bible, New
International Version®*. *NIV®*. Copyright © 1973, 1978, 1984 by International Bible
Society. Used by permission of Zondervan. All rights reserved. Scripture quotations
marked NASB are taken from the *New American Standard Bible*, © Copyright 1960,
1995 by The Lockman Foundation. Used by permission. Scripture quotations marked
KJV are taken from the King James Version of the Bible. (Public Domain.) Scripture
quotations marked MSG are taken from *THE MESSAGE*. Copyright © by Eugene
H. Peterson 1993, 1994, 1995, 1996, 2000, 2001, 2002. Used by permission of
NavPress Publishing Group. The author has added italics to quotations for emphasis.

LCCN 2009910649
ISBN: 978-1-4347-6726-4
eISBN: 978-1-4347-0084-1

The Team: Susan Tjaden, Sarah Schultz, Caitlyn York, Karen Athen
Cover Photo: Strong Tower Photography
Cover Design: Amy Kiechlin

Printed in the United States of America
First Edition 2010

1 2 3 4 5 6 7 8 9 10

113009

Luke,

If the fact I've just finished a book giving advice to ministry wives isn't sidesplitting hilarious, I don't know what is. This baby is definitely my Isaac. I don't know that anyone can fully appreciate the irony and laugh along with me except for you, my husband and best friend. You know above anyone else how much we never saw this coming. You also know what a sweet ride this life has been. Of all the ways God could have chosen to define me, I will forever be grateful that He made me the wife of a pastor and the mother of the four most amazing preacher's kids. I would live every moment of it all over again.

Thank you for releasing me to do the things God has asked of me—especially when it means you eat grilled cheese sandwiches for supper instead of gourmet Hamburger Helper. One day we'll be feasting at Jesus' table, and something tells me it will never be disappointing. I hope I've made it up in other ways, though I can't think of what those are just this minute. I suppose the fact I don't deserve you is why I remain humbled that God gave you to me anyway.

> *In his heart a man plans his course,*
> *but the LORD determines his steps. (Prov. 16:9)*

I love you!

Lisa

CONTENTS

FOREWORD

I first discovered Lisa McKay in the blog world. My daughter, who is also a pastor's wife, had found Lisa's online encouragement refreshing. She thought I'd enjoy it too. Little did I know that I'd soon discover a new online friend.

No, Lisa and I have never met in person. We've communicated through our blogs and the occasional email, but for the most part our "friendship" has developed because of her communication style. She's down-to-earth, honest, and vulnerable. Her humor and wit help keep everyday ministry challenges in perspective.

Every pastor's wife needs a friend like Lisa. We all need to be around other women who understand what our lives are like. Thanks to the publishing world, Lisa will now be that friend for thousands of pastor's wives. Lisa has taken the time to share the wisdom she has learned from years of life in the fishbowl. It's time for a fresh voice for pastor's wives, and Lisa is just that voice.

I've been a pastor's wife for over twenty years. I've raised five children in the public eye. I've served as a pastor's wife in a church of three thousand and in a church of two hundred. The dynamics are different, but the challenges are the same. People are people wherever you go. And ministry is all about people. As a pastor's wife, I've experienced joy in having a front-row seat to watch God work. I've also cried tears of hurt and frustration. Both are experiences that you've likely experienced as well. Those are the highs and lows of ministry.

In *You Can Still Wear Cute Shoes,* Lisa touches on all the aspects of ministry life. This book is like having a girlfriend in your back pocket. And if there's anything that ministry wives need, it's a good girlfriend! If you are a ministry wife, I promise you will be encouraged. If you are part of a church and know a pastor's wife, I guarantee you will be enlightened.

Fix yourself a cup of coffee, curl up in a comfy chair, and spend some time with Lisa McKay. You, your family, and your church will be better because you did.

Jill Savage
Author of *Real Moms ... Real Jesus* and CEO of Hearts at Home

ACKNOWLEDGMENTS

Dear reader, you hold in your hand the product of the hardest thing I've ever done short of birthing children. This book was written poolside, playground-side, and in various rooms in my home to a steady soundtrack of *SpongeBob SquarePants* and *Hannah Montana*. There were many days I didn't think I could finish, but I've learned afresh that God is not keen on abandoning a good work He's begun.

In giving thanks, I have to bow first to my Savior and King, Jesus Christ. You know I never asked to be a preacher's wife and certainly never considered myself worthy to presume advising others. Only You know the reason You orchestrated every perfectly timed detail that produced this book. Only You know why You chose me to give courage to the women who faithfully serve You by upholding their minister husbands. Your body is precious to me, and I love You for allowing me to be a pinkie toe in it.

Luke, Sawyer, Elijah, Sam, and Sydney—I wish we had a nickel for every time during this process that I said, "Does this sound goofy?" or "Guys, can you please just give me a few more minutes of quiet?" I also wish I had one for every time you said, "You can do this, honey!" or "It's kinda cool to have a mom who's writing a book." Though it goes without saying, you guys are pretty cool too.

To all my parents—it seems I got most of the words in our family. Thank you for teaching me to use them and being patient while I did.

Pop—you taught me to laugh from the deeps. You truly were my Barnabas, and I still miss you every day.

Grandmommy—your love for the written word and skill for storytelling always bound me to you. I think you would be proud to have another bona fide author in the family.

To John Blase—I'm so happy you read girl blogs and that somehow God led you to mine. Thank you for seeing something I didn't and for refusing to settle on a title that was less than perfection.

To Don Pape—blessings on you for taking a chance on a small-town preacher's wife. I will always keep the email in which you used the phrase "Da Bomb." It sealed you in my heart forever.

Susan Tjaden—I never dreamed a day would come when I could use the words *my* and *editor* in the same sentence. What is even more unimaginable is that I can also add *friend* to the mix. Jesus knows my insecurities and sent me someone who has been a gigantic serving of encouragement with a side order of belly laughs. I can never thank you enough for using your enormous skill to make my work look better. Much love to you, my editor friend.

Bonnie Bruno—when we met, ours were two out of eight million blogs on WordPress. That the Lord crossed our paths seems a statistical impossibility, and yet you appeared and began nudging and coaching and loving me into writing with purpose. You are a mentor like no other. And since we've never spoken on the phone,

I'm not altogether sure you aren't an angel. What a silly thing to wonder—of course you are.

Linda Attaway—you complete me with your affinity for details. Thank you for volunteering to clean up my messes.

And finally, my darling fellow ministry wives—your insight through my many blog surveys was invaluable in creating the content for this book. I've done my best to give you God's Word in answer to many issues we face. Each of you is precious to me, and it is my desire above all things that you will walk away from this volume assured that God wasn't mad at you when he made your husband a pastor. He has entrusted you with tending to His body, which means you, girls, are *special*. Remembering that will help you love His people well.

INTRODUCTION

"God is calling you to do *what?*"

Such was my reaction fifteen years ago when my husband, Luke, told me he felt God was leading him into the gospel ministry. Even though I supported him wholeheartedly, I naively believed this calling was somehow just his gig. My job was simply to accompany him while he did his "thing."

Reality didn't hit until a well-meaning gentleman enlightened me on the expectations of a minister's wife. He said, "The best thing you can do for Luke is learn how to play the piano. He'll have a much easier time being called as a pastor of a church. Congregations love it when the pastor's wife can contribute. It's like they are getting two for one!" If I knew then what I know now, I would have had a serious fight with the flesh to keep from sharing my thoughts on the buy-one-get-one-free concept.

The restraint of the Holy Spirit is a beautiful thing.

Before that moment, it truly had not entered my mind that anyone would expect anything of me, or that my lack of musical talent could affect my husband's "success" in ministry. I thought of my childhood pastor's wife, a grim-faced woman whose hair was piled high in a bun. Polyester skirts and sensible shoes were her standard uniform. And, yes, she played the piano. Was this the person I must become in order for God to use our family in ministry?

Talk about an Extreme Makeover!

We moved to Kentucky so Luke could attend Bible college. The first thing I did was to begin comparing myself to every woman on campus who no doubt was doing the exact same thing. The question we were all asking ourselves? "What in the world does a preacher's wife do?" Our husbands were getting an education on how to become ministers while we were left to wonder how we figured into the equation. I found my answer in an overzealous, pharisaic overhaul of the externals. I began wearing clothes I wouldn't have been caught dead in before—mostly suited for three times my twenty-two years of age. I tamed my '80s hair. I calmed my type A personality by yielding in conversation and becoming more reserved. I baked casseroles for every surgery and every baby born. The word that guided my reinvention was *Martha*. Not the Martha of Scripture, mind you, but Martha Stewart. (Now that I think of it, there isn't much difference, is there?)

It also did not help that the books I read about being a ministry wife only reinforced my insecurities. The advice ranged from how to brew a perfect cup of tea for a ladies' luncheon to how to organize a large staff when hosting a dinner party. According to these books, I was to be gracious at all times, keep a spotless home, and have well-dressed, obedient children. I'm certainly not criticizing these noble aspirations, but even before children I was completely overwhelmed at this picture of perfection. I don't agree with the busyness of our culture, yet there is no use in denying I often fall prey to its trappings. The truth is, I am a wife and mother deep in the trenches. The only tea I brew is Lipton. And staff? Are you kidding me? If I ever have a workforce at my disposal, they will be too busy doing laundry to prepare a dinner for the deacons. And where do I begin with the kids? Someone please tell me what to do with a child who sneaks his Halloween costume under his clothes, strips off in the bathroom, and shakes hands as Spiderman during the greeting song when he is supposed to be in children's church. Susanna Wesley would definitely not approve.

I can laugh now at all the crazy things I thought back in the day and the pressure I put on myself and my family to be perfect, only because I've done my time with the tears brought on by unrealistic expectations from myself and others. It has taken years, but I thank God for helping me recognize that my most important role is as a helpmate to Luke and a loving mother to our children. In the midst of molding me into a godlier wife and mom, He has also placed the calling of minister's wife on my life, and thankfully nowhere in Scripture does it say I have to play the piano, wear polyester, or host the perfect party.

I wish I could give you a list of requirements that would make you a great preacher's wife. The truth is, the obedience required in exercising our individual gifts makes that list a very organic thing that changes from one woman to the other. However, understanding that we have many common experiences, there are many practical things I have learned that I wish someone had told me in the beginning. I can't help but think I wasted a lot of time worrying about what I appeared to be instead of cultivating the gifts God gave the woman I truly was. I could have avoided many a broken heart had I known the difference between true friendship and selfish motivations. I could have saved my kids some undue pressure by not placing the same yoke of expectation on them that was a burden to me. I could have been a better support to my husband by realizing Satan would attack his ministry close to home.

In addition to addressing these topics and more, this book will also give you insight from other ministry wives who understand the delights and difficulties you face. One of the things we tend to lack most is a "safe" friendship where we can pour our hearts out without the fear of repercussion to someone walking our same road. Near the end of each chapter, you will find a "Round Table," which contains advice and comments from other women serving alongside their husbands in capacities ranging from the senior pastorate to music ministry to evangelism. These are excerpts from conversations on my blog, The Preacher's Wife (www.APreachersWife.com), where I invite you to visit for fresh, relevant discussions on ministry and other fun topics. The end of this book includes several computer links and resources to help you further explore the online community and camaraderie available.

Our worldwide locations and denominations influence our role "titles." Whether you are the preacher's wife, the pastor's wife, the vicar's wife, or the wife of a man serving in some other area of ministry, I want you to hear my heart when I tell you I've prayed diligently for you during the writing of this book. I've asked God to show me Scripture that will guide you through the many common complexities we share. I've asked Him to reveal His heart to you and that the experiences I share will resonate with your own. I've begged

Him to let this book be one that will give you righteous confidence in the leadership role He has given you in your home and church.

By sharing what I've learned as the wife of a minister, I hope to save you from the pitfalls I've experienced. To spare you a few years of trial and error in relating to those you serve, to guard you from a few heartaches, and to let you know you are not alone. To convince you that your unique gifts and personality can translate into one fantastic pastor's wife whether or not you are an outgoing hostess, your flower beds are weeded, or you and the kids are on time for Sunday school. I pray with all my heart that you know these chapters overflow with a deep affection for those of you who are married to the ministry.

One

MY HUSBAND'S CALLING
IS MY CALLING TOO

Many are the plans in a man's heart,
but it is the LORD's purpose that prevails.
—*Proverbs 19:21*

I once had an interesting conversation with a woman whose husband had enrolled in seminary to prepare for ministry. "He can take classes all he wants, but I didn't sign up for the preacher's wife thing," she said. Since she didn't believe her husband would actually follow through, she went on to tell me she planned on humoring him until the day his calling affected her. And if that day ever came? Well, she'd just cross that bridge when she came to it.

He is still in school. She is still in denial.

Around that same time I attended a pastors' wives conference that included a panel discussion at the end. Lined across the stage, five women in different seasons of ministry shared the thing they found most difficult about being married to a minister.

I'll never forget the response of the youngest woman. She was a mom of toddlers and was obviously distressed. "The hardest thing for me is everyone wanting a piece of my husband and not acknowledging me in the least," she said. "I feel like the person in the background who is only here to take care of the kids so he can be free to take care of everyone else."

I was grieved by her raw response. All I wanted to do was wrap my arms around that girl and assure her she had it all wrong. That she was an integral part of her husband's ministry. That her calling in that season was her children. That no amount of public success possibly mattered if her heart and home were in shambles. The sad thing is that I've met many more like her in the past fifteen years during my own life as a minister's wife. If anything, this has intensified my desire to embrace and encourage women whom God has charged with supporting the men He has ordained to proclaim His Word.

The fact that I just typed that last sentence still baffles me. You have no idea how surreal it is for me to be writing this book. There are many of you reading who have been Christians as long as you can remember and always knew you would marry a preacher. Many more of you grew up as the child of a minister and swore you would never marry one yourself, only to find yourself eating your words. Some of you have pursued callings to various vocational ministries and met your mate in college, seminary, etc. Some of you married men who were already serving in the church. However, based on my blog surveys, a lot of your serene lives were turned inside out when your husband experienced God's call to ministry some point after you were married.

And then on the lunatic fringe are girls like me whose life and marital background weren't exactly résumé worthy.

A Match Made in Heaven?

My husband, Luke, and I married young. I was a mere eighteen and he a strapping twenty-one. Can I just be honest and tell you there were never two individuals any more needy or any less likely to be serving behind a pulpit?

I always cringe when we run into old high school friends. The question of what we're doing now always comes up, and there is one response that we can count on when we share that Luke is a pastor—after the laughter dies down, that is.

"Luke, *you* are a preacher? And Lisa? *You* are a preacher's *wife?!* Okay, joke's over. Now what are you *really* doing?"

We would be offended if we weren't just as baffled.

I forgive our flabbergasted friends because I can't hold their excellent recall against them. They remember the dangerous combination of the wild boy and the bitter girl whose marriage was tumultuous at best. Surely, the future they envisioned for us was set in a divorce court rather than a sanctuary. They were within days of being absolutely correct.

There is no human reason why Luke and I should still be wed today, much less serving the body of Christ. Even though we were not yet believers, our union started off well enough. But we soon faced the heartbreaking yet all too common reality of many young couples: The stress of working different shifts, having more month than money, and living the separate lives that developed in the midst of it resulted in our parting ways and filing for divorce two short years after the ceremony.

I *despised* the not-yet-preacher, and the truth is I loathed myself as much as him. We had hurt each other in a million ways, and all I could think of was getting away and starting over. We were within a week of our divorce being final when one night I received a bizarre phone call from him. He told me he had started going to church again and wanted us to rethink what we were doing.

I went off the deep end! I spewed, "So you are turning into a religious fanatic—and you think that is going to fix everything?" I was so full of hate and bitterness, and it still makes me blush to think of all the horrible things I said to him about his newfound religion. He continued, very patiently, to call and tell me he was asking God for a miracle as the clock ticked toward the day our marriage would be legally over.

One night during that critical week before the divorce was final, I had gone to bed, still convinced divorce was the only answer. For some reason, I woke up around two and the tears began to flow. I missed my husband so badly I could barely lie there. I remember thinking, "What is wrong with you? You cannot stand him! It's almost over, just hang in there." I realize now that voice was Satan's, bent on thwarting God's plan for us. If you ask me how I know prayer works or how I know God can turn a cold heart into one that can feel love, laughter, and joy (Ezek. 11:19), I will point you to that night because it is the one that changed everything.

I called Luke the next day. One conversation led to another, and we called the lawyer to stop the divorce proceedings. I tentatively moved back home with Luke, and we began visiting churches. I was still not very thrilled about the "God thing," but I knew for some reason I wanted my husband back and this would play a part. Would it ever!

One night soon afterward, my hubby came to me in our living room and told me he had just prayed for salvation. He'd gone to church his whole life, but it was only at that time he truly accepted Christ as his Savior. I grew up in a totally different denomination, so this Baptist way of doing things was a little traumatic for me. I was glad for him, but I still wasn't so sure what that meant for me. For personal reasons, organized religion held no real appeal, so I was very afraid of how my husband's becoming so radically different was going to affect me and our life together. Seemingly out of the blue, I began having feelings of not being good enough for this new man, and shame over my own sin slowly entered my heart.

For me, salvation was not a lightning-bolt experience but rather an intellectual process at first. I needed to *understand* it. First Corinthians 1:18 says, "For the message of the cross is foolishness to those who are perishing, but to us who are being saved it is the power of God." I know the Spirit of God enabled me to believe what I was hearing because obviously I could have still walked away a scoffer. We were attending my husband's childhood church, and the pastor became a dear friend and mentor to us both. He started a small group in his home, and I was able to ask all my questions in a very nonthreatening environment. That man was very patient with me as I asked everything from "What does 'once saved, always saved' mean?" to "When do you think the rapture will happen?" Sometime in the midst of those sessions, I realized I had already made a decision. That decision was for life—both for Jesus Christ and until-death-do-us-part with my husband. I asked the Lord to "officially" save me and soon afterward made that public in the body of people who had prayed so faithfully for us both.

If this had been the end of the story I would have been happily-ever-after indeed. Little did I know our tale was only beginning.

The Call

Over the next weeks, I watched Luke transform in front of my eyes. Where once stood a rough-around-the-edges construction worker, I now found a softened gentleman. Where turmoil had churned, peace now reigned. A thirst for the world was replaced by an unquenchable longing to drink up every bit of the Word that he'd neglected for the past years.

I'm in no way suggesting that a called minister is on a plane above any other Christian, but what I will say is that even in my own spiritually immature state, what I saw happening in Luke seemed to be so much more fervent than what I saw in other men. And as for my own walk, Luke's desire made me long for more. If I can be so biased, Luke was special—an opinion I still hold.

I tell you this because I want you to understand that after Luke finally told me he believed God was calling him to minister, my head was shocked, but my heart wasn't. Something in me perceived our life had taken a twist that surpassed simply returning to our old lives as a renewed version of our previous selves. We both were experiencing intense restlessness in our jobs. I had just left an entire career on a lark. And Luke, who had always loved his trade and coworkers, began dreading the alarm clock every morning.

Have you ever read the book *The Return of the King* in The Lord of the Rings trilogy? In the end Frodo the hobbit leaves his home, the Shire, after risking his life to save it. When explaining to his best friend, Sam, why he has to go, he says, "There is no real going back. Though I may come to the Shire, it will not seem the same; for I shall not be the same." In much the same way, the dailiness of our lives had taken on a sense of not quite belonging in the place that had always been familiar. Accepting the fact that God was calling us to serve Him in some capacity was like turning a dial to the last number on a combination lock. The "rightness" of it clicked, and suddenly the future was wide open.

Sign, Sign, Everywhere a Sign

Luke and I began to pray and seek God for what He wanted us to do—definitely a first in our married lives. I have no biblical basis for what I am going to say next, but I believe God answers the prayers of baby Christians with a shout instead of a whisper. God has taught us how to discern Him more through prayer and His Word now, but in those early days He had to throw up the flashing neon signs before our own lightbulbs lit up.

The first two of those signs were named Al and Doyle. Both of these men mentioned the name of Clear Creek Baptist Bible College within two days of one another. Al had just returned from a Constructors for Christ project, during which they had built new one-bedroom duplexes for married students without children. Doyle was a longtime supporter of the school. These days I call that type of communication from God a double affirmation, but then we were still thinking, "Hmmm.… That's odd. I wonder if we are supposed to look into this."

And God was saying, "Ya think?" while restraining Himself from knocking our foolish heads together.

Luke hesitated contacting the school to request information because he had no hopes of getting in. What I've not yet told you is that he didn't graduate high school. What dropout had any kind of chance to go to college? He finally mustered the nerve to call, and we scheduled a visit. We still didn't know for what. Both of us realized we wouldn't be able to go right away but thought maybe the school could give some pointers on what Luke could do to become a student someday.

We traveled to the college and were in love at first sight. The campus was set in the mountains and was absolute lush, peaceful perfection. Arriving there felt like coming home, which at the time was heartbreaking because we knew this place couldn't possibly be in our near future.

The following day we met the director of admissions, Jay. He was and remains one of the most boisterous, joyful, encouraging people we have ever known. Luke explained his full situation—particularly the part about not having a diploma. Luke expected to hear, "Sorry, son, but you don't belong here. Come back in a year or two when you are good enough." Instead Jay chuckled and said, "No problem!"

No problem? How is not having a high school diploma not a problem?

Brother Jay enthusiastically went on to explain there was a special program in this college for men who did not have a high school degree. They would take regular college courses and also be tutored for high school in the freshman year. Students had two semesters to pass the GED, at which point they would have official student status and all classes would count toward a fully accredited degree.

And just like that, there was Neon Sign Three, and it blinked wildly, "Road Open!"

Our patient, gracious God gave us three signs in an overwhelming answer to our many prayers—and they all pointed toward our new home. (One of the homes Al built, no less!)

Absolutely Certain (I Think)

Well, enough about us—for now anyway! Since I've shared a little backstory with you, I'd like to talk about what I believe is one of the foundational principles of our lives as ministry wives: the nature of our own call.

I realize each of our inductions into a life of ministry was met with different levels of enthusiasm. It's not every woman who looks forward to low salaries and high expectations. Of frequent moves and misunderstood children. Of criticism and conflict. These are just a few stereotypical pitfalls that can understandably cause a woman to put the skids on any plans her man has for serving in vocational ministry.

As Luke was processing the call God placed on his life, I was blessedly ignorant of all the things I just listed. My church experience was limited to a few years of attendance as a child, so I really had no comprehension of the chew-'em-up-and-spit-'em-out reputation of churches where ministers are concerned. Naïveté is not always a bad thing—especially when knowing all the details could result in being too fearful to take the leap into God's plan for your future.

But what part do you play in what God is asking your husband to do? Has God called you in the same manner as him? My short answer is to state plainly that every wife has the God-given role of being a faithful helpmate no matter if her husband is a banker, a mechanic, or a schoolteacher. However, there are unique challenges and more assured uncertainties for the wife who has the high charge of supporting a man directed to leave the familiar behind and follow God's call into the unknown. What are some of those challenges, and how should we who find ourselves in this situation react? Let's learn from someone who has gone before us— Abraham's wife, Sarah.

A Woman Out of Control

We meet Sarah (Sarai) in Genesis 11:29 and in verse 30 are told simply, "[She] was barren; she had no children." In the Middle Eastern culture, Sarah's dignity was directly tied to her being married and having babies. Since she was childless, she would not have risked staying behind without her husband, no matter how unsure she may have been about Abraham asking her to leave Ur. There was nothing but shame for Sarah in Ur without Abraham.

And conversely, there was nothing in Canaan for Abraham without Sarah. It was out of Sarah's infertility that God would perform one of His most awesome works—the miraculous birth of a nation consecrated to Himself. Abraham could have found any number of women who weren't suffering from the heartbreak of barrenness to be his wife. However, the supernatural birth of Isaac was the requirement for properly illustrating God's glory through human hopelessness.

Long before Abraham met Sarah, God purposed for the two of them to be the human agents through whom He would bless the nations. Neither of them could have participated in God's plan alone—each needed the other. That concept is no different for those God continues to call today to spread the good news throughout the world.

When I think of all the quirks and hang-ups that Luke and I both have, it is amazing to realize that for the most part we do not have the same ones. Luke is painfully shy; I'm the social extrovert. Luke is compassionate to a fault, whereas I am more critical. Luke doesn't understand drama, and I am a master of it; therefore, I am able to help him comprehend the underlying issues women have when he has no clue how to proceed. God placed us together as a team to complement one another's weaknesses and to nurture the spiritual children He has entrusted to our care. I have total and complete faith in Luke's ability and he in mine, and yet neither of us believes for a second we could have any measure of ministry success without the support of the other.

To the reluctant ministry wife, I understand your fear. I know your need to have some input on how and where you are going to raise your family. Even the wondrous event of God entering into covenant with Abraham on the assurance of an heir was not enough to keep Sarah from trying to control the way in which the promised child would come into the world. And thirteen years later, Sarah laughed when they were told once again she would have a son. Abraham's seed could be reckoned only through Sarah, and that required a separate faith on her part—a willing participation in what God purposed to accomplish through their son, Isaac. Sarah wasn't perfect. She could be harsh and unbelieving and manipulative. However, Hebrews 11:11 tells us God gave her strength to participate in the creation and blessing of nations because "she considered Him faithful who had promised" (NASB).

My personal feeling is that we can make the idea of serving in ministry way more complex than God ever intended. In the case of Abraham, God promised children more numerous than the stars in the sky and the sands on the seashore, but He didn't ask him to father them all! He gave Abraham charge over one piece of that promise— beloved Isaac. Sometimes we can get so caught up in the enormity of what God is asking us to do that we forget the Big Picture is composed of individual frames of obedience. I'm guilty of shutting down physically and mentally when the job seems way too big—and all God has asked of me is to trust Him one day at a time. It's much easier to walk into the unknown if we can focus on being faithful with what is required of us today, trusting God for His faithfulness in all our tomorrows.

It's Simple, Really

Are we called alongside our husbands? Absolutely. Is the life we are called to complex? You bet. But, based on my personal experience and the example of Sarah, I believe we are asked to do three things that will simplify our thinking and therefore help us not only to accept but also to look forward to a certain future.

We are called to trust.

First Peter 3:6 says, "Just as Sarah obeyed Abraham, calling him lord, ... you have become her children if you do what is right without being frightened by any fear" (NASB).

This verse is found in a passage describing how a woman's beauty is to be found internally instead of externally (verses 1–5). Among other things, Peter describes how a woman should be in willing subjection to her husband, even if he is not a believer. Dread shouldn't motivate her in yielding to him, but rather a healthy fear of God's mandate to honor her husband. Sarah's singular obedience was dually blessed. She wanted to obey God by following Abraham. God's laws are not arbitrary and are not given without benefit attached. Sarah's reward was the gift of inclusion into the blessing of the nations that God had intended through Abraham. If we seek to surrender our lives to God's will through His call on our husbands, we will be given the blessed distinction of being a daughter of Sarah.

So what does this type of obedience look like in a minister's wife? Certainly the amount of reluctance you are feeling toward this role will dictate the type of faith it will take to accompany your husband into the unknown. Hear me well when I say that no matter how much initial trepidation I feel when God asks something of our family, He has yet to call Luke to a task without also piercing my own heart. It is always heartbreaking for me to talk to ministry wives who do not express any sense of calling toward their husband's work. The reasons are endless, but most often the wife incorrectly believes that his ministry is just another vocation and has nothing to do with her, or she absolutely wants nothing to do with a life with trappings holding no obvious appeal.

You may ask, "Is it wrong if I don't want my husband to be a preacher? Can anyone blame me if I don't want to leave what is comfortable and predictable? What if I don't want to move away from my extended family?" And bigger still, "What if I don't trust my husband to discern God's voice?"

If you find yourself feeling this way, then it is time to look past your wants and even those of your husband and straight to the face of God. Ask Him what He requires of you. Are you willing to trust Him with your unknown? Are you willing to obey even if you believe your man has some static in his radio? I wish I had an easy answer here, but in reality these questions can be hashed out only in some sincere facedown time with the Father. Because I continually remember the comfort and reassurance He has offered me with these same fears, I can promise you He'll invade your heart with a much-needed peace in the midst of the pain that often goes along with hard-fought obedience.

Luke and I had no idea in the beginning what our exact ministry would look like. Would we be missionaries? Would he be behind a pulpit? Would we work in a parachurch organization? We had no clue. In the same way, be assured you won't always know every detail of what God is asking of you. However, though the *what* may be unclear, we can always trust the motivation of the *Who*. Our faith in His promises and the assurance of His continual blessing upon the nations through our obedience in spreading His Word is enough to follow our man wherever God leads.

We are called to participate.

Hebrews 11:11–12 says, "By faith even Sarah herself received ability to conceive, even beyond the proper time of life, since she considered Him faithful who had promised. Therefore there was born even of one man, and him as good as dead at that, as many descendants as the stars of heaven in number, and innumerable as the sand which is by the seashore" (NASB).

I can identify with Sarah on so many levels. Though she is heralded as a model of faithfulness, we know she behaved badly in her doubt. Just think about her side for a bit. God made these covenant promises to Abraham but never mentioned Sarah's name once until she was ninety years old—some twenty-five years after God first appeared to her husband. She knew God promised Abraham an heir, and when the plan she hatched to speed that along resulted in Hagar's pregnancy, Sarah may have felt left out by God entirely.

Are you like the girl in the beginning of this chapter who felt no one needed her? Do you ever feel left behind to cook, clean, and take care of babies while your husband spends the better part of his days ministering to everyone but you? Are you convinced he is having a blast crusading for the kingdom while you are stuck at home in the castle—as Cinderella no less?

Obviously the season of life you are in dictates to what degree you are able to participate in the work of the church. Listen closely, young mothers! Your ministry in this stage of life is to those precious babies in your care. If you have your own desires to serve in things such as women's ministry, Bible study, administration, etc., your day will come. Some of you are able to soldier on and do these things in addition to caring for your toddlers, but many are just not able to do it all. And you know what? You aren't supposed to. If you find your home is suffering and your kids are begging for your attention, then they—not church ministry—take absolute precedence. Never, ever apologize for making your family first!

My children are no longer babies, but I am just as busy with them in other ways. Diaper changing and bottle feeding have given way to homework and taxi service to whatever sport they are playing at the moment. Though I consider myself active in ministry, there are many things I don't do. For example, I don't always make it to the funeral home every time someone passes, due to the simple fact that I would have to bring my kids and I don't particularly think they enjoy going any more than I enjoy having to get them dressed and wrangling them once there. I do have a trade-off, however—I help with the meal if we are hosting one for the grieving family. The kids can hang out in a back room, and the stress is greatly relieved for them and for me. Not to mention our darling church ladies always fix the kids a plate from the leftovers. This is my way of letting the family know I love them, I care, and I am taking part to the best of my current ability without making myself crazy.

No matter if you are a seasoned ministry wife or a relative newbie, there is always one thing your congregation will pick up on loud and clear—your willingness to serve despite your inability.

Do you work outside the home but do your best to participate in the body when possible? The church knows this and for the most part will understand. (Oh, there will always be exceptions!)

However, what they will not easily forgive is when you take a seat in the back and refuse to play a part—able or not. There are many women who are embittered by the demands the church has placed on their family's life and time; therefore they refuse to support their husband's ministry or the church body in any way, shape, or form. We'll discuss in a later chapter the delicate balance between home and church life, but let's just say for now that this attitude is extremely unhealthy and can be a huge detriment to your husband's relationship with the church. The support the congregation perceives your husband receiving from you and your willingness to care for them even if you aren't able to do all that you'd like is a bridge between their hearts and your man's. Just like Sarah and Abraham's situation, your participation in his call is not only nice but necessary for him to effectively live out what God will do through him, whether you realize it now or not.

We are called to hope.

A life in ministry ultimately calls us to one thing: a hope for a greater glory than current circumstances reveal. I can't think of a higher charge than the invitation to participate in God's good intentions toward His creation. Sarah considered God faithful in His promises toward her, and because of that, she was able to look past the difficult years of childlessness and hold the manifestation of God's blessing in her own arms.

Many years ago I watched a mafia movie (I don't have any idea what it was called) where a gangster was teaching his young son about trust. The boy was on a ladder, and the father repeatedly told him to fall backward into his arms: "Don't worry! I'm your father. Do you really think I'd let you be hurt?" The boy was more frightened of his dad than the fall, so he let go of the ladder. As he fell the dad stepped to the side and let him crash to the ground. His son stared up in surprised pain as the father said, "Never trust anyone."

I think many of us have the mind-set that God is the father who is setting us up for a huge fall and that we can't trust Him to keep something painful from happening to us. The difference is He is standing in your unknown saying, "You can *always* trust me!"

He never promises our lives won't hurt, but you know what? He will always cushion us. Certainly there are hard days, but in the midst of them you will find laughter, just like Abraham and Sarah did. Sometimes those giggles you share will be born out of pure joy and at other times from incredulous disbelief. The thing to always remember is that you and your husband are in this thing together. There is no part of what God intends to do through either of you that isn't intimately intertwined with the love and support of the other. God has appointed your husband according to his gifts, and your first priority as his wife is to affirm him in this role. However, many of you have desires for ministry that will involve taking off in your own direction. That doesn't mean you supplant your hubby, but in the appropriate season, there will be many ways in which your own talents will broaden the scope of what he is able to do alongside you versus going it alone.

If You Say So

One of the coolest things about this book is the fact that these are not just my own observations! I mentioned in the introduction that I have a blog called The Preacher's Wife (www.APreachersWife.com). Blogs are explained in greater detail in Appendix B of this book.

As part of the research for this project I asked a series of survey questions to the ministry wives who hang out with me online. (I'm excited to tell you there are a lot of them!) These Round Table discussions provide advice and encouragement from women who are serving in the trenches just like you. More than anything, I pray this book confirms the fact you are not alone in your circumstances, your joys, your struggles, or your opinions. I am so thrilled to introduce you to an online community of women who absolutely understand where you are coming from. I've also gathered comments from laypeople. I think it is imperative that we hear from both perspectives in order to understand one another's hearts and hopefully build stronger relationships.

Now let me be clear: I am in no way saying that "virtual" friends should replace your flesh-and-blood ones. What I can tell you is that I have met many women in person whom I've first made contact with online through my blog, and they've become my dearest confidantes. Blogs are but one fresh and relevant way to establish connections with women who will support you in your role as a ministry wife. We'll discuss those various avenues in a later chapter centered on friendships.

For ease of identification (and to show off my excessive-texting-abbreviation skills), my blog friends will be known as the M2M Girls (as in, Married to Ministry Girls). Make sense? Let's see what they had to share about their perspectives on calling.

Round Table

- "I never wanted to be a pastor's wife. When my husband felt called (before we got engaged) I had doubts. But, what God wanted and had planned was far greater than I knew at the time. He eventually convinced my heart to follow Him."—Sarah @ Life in the Parsonage

- "I feel like my highest calling is to be my husband's supporter, his encourager, his helpmate. I believe that my service in the home, especially at this season in our lives with small children, is the biggest call in that ministry. He could not focus on doing the greatest part of his calling—preaching the gospel—if I didn't do mine."—Crystal @ Life Is Nothing Without Him

- "As a layperson, I think it is obvious when a wife doesn't share her husband's passion for ministry. I don't believe a pastor's wife has to be everyone's friend or attend every church event. But I do think you can tell by her general demeanor if she is ministry-minded. And, rightly or wrongly, the vibe I get from her reflects on her husband."—Lori (layperson)

- "I felt a call to ministry years before I met my husband, and deep down I hoped that call meant I would marry a minister. My challenge came several years later when he started thinking about leaving the ministry and I thought, 'Wait a minute. I married you as a minister, so you have to stay one!' I came to realize that I was married to him—a person, not his title—and I would love him no matter what."—Kecia @ Kecia's Journey

- "I don't know of any other occupation that my husband could have that would require me to be a part of the 'package deal' (for free) except the ministry. That took some getting used to!"—Sherry @ Life at the Parsonage

- "It's easy to spot a woman who's happy for and proud of her husband's life/accomplishments/calling. It may not be easy for her to 'follow' when she is in the background with young children (early on), but she is proud of her man's walk and character. That is a beautiful thing to see."—Darnelle (layperson) @ All Things Work Together

Now That You Know:

1. How are you responding to God's call on your husband? Seek out a seasoned pastor's wife and ask her to share her experience with you for reassurance.

2. Take the power away from the vague fears Satan will give you about the uncertainties you face by writing down what scares you. Search out the truth of God's Word to apply to each. Afraid of moving away from family? Claim Matthew 19:29. Worried your family will not be provided for? Pray Psalm 37:25.

3. Laypeople: Has a man in your congregation announced a call to ministry? He is often congratulated and much is made over his decision, but his wife may be struggling in his shadow. Take the time to encourage her by pointing out the gifts she has that will be an asset to him. If there isn't a new minister in your midst, consider writing a note of encouragement to your existing pastor's wife to let her know what a vital part she plays in her husband's work.

Two

I CAN STILL WEAR CUTE SHOES

Today you are you! That is truer than true!
There is no one alive who is you-er than you!
—*Dr. Seuss,* Happy Birthday to You!

When considering what I will call my personal Fashion Evolution, I must first tell you that the last time I was in vogue was May of 1989. That would be the month and year of my high school graduation. Just so we can be clear on how "in style" I was, my '80s paisley pants, leg warmers, and shoe jewels landed me the Best Dressed of my senior class.

Yes, I was quite the fashionista.

Fast-forward a year. Luke and I were very young newlyweds, and unfortunately paying the light bill always trumped my need for a new outfit. Financial pressures increased, and the more time passed, the more dated my wardrobe became. This was particularly distressing to me because my clothes were one of the ways I expressed my type A personality.

I have already shared our salvation story and later call to ministry, but before that time there were things God was allowing to happen in my life that brought me to the place of realizing I needed Him—desperately. It seems shallow, perhaps, to equate my clothing woes with the downward spiral of my life, but what I was wearing represented what my heart was feeling. In short, I was losing touch and losing control—in life and in clothes. I believe now that this discontentment of soul, this feeling that my identity was fading, was just one of the catalysts God used to draw me to Him. I'll refer you back to my testimony as a reminder of how my almost failed marriage was an essential piece of my realizing I needed salvation. But for now I want to focus on my immediate reaction to Luke's call to ministry after these times passed.

The New Me

I'm assuming it's obvious that in those early days clothing was a way to communicate who I was as an individual and that most likely, you can relate. So when Luke told me he felt God had called him to ministry—and especially after we moved away to attend Bible college—I became preoccupied with the question, "What in the world is a preacher's wife supposed to wear?"

It was exciting, actually, this whole idea of a personal reinvention. If Madonna could do it, couldn't I? (In a decidedly more conservative way, of course.) No one told me that twenty-two was a little young to go looking for this new identity in the Misses department (aka Where My Grandmother Shops). However, I knew Gap was off-limits because, in my estimation, a proper preacher's wife shouldn't be caught dead in anything described as hip or trendy.

I still have no idea what possessed me the day I went shopping and managed to migrate from leggings with an oversized tunic to my first birdhouse-embroidered sweater and elastic-waist slacks. (Slacks! That word still makes me cringe!) To complete the look, I purchased a pair of sensible loafers. I was swollen with pride to have found something that made me look so *religious* and couldn't wait to get home so I could model this new outfit for Luke.

As I twirled around amid the birds and kittens on my fetching little cardigan, I asked him one of the most dangerous questions a wife can pose to her husband: "How do I look?" Without a moment's hesitation he answered with the fail-safe phrase every guy keeps tucked away for such a time as this: "That's nice, honey." (Luke is such a trooper. He smiled graciously right through the look of confusion on his face.) I remember feeling transformed as I looked at this new woman in the mirror. One pleasing word came to mind—*appropriate.*

And that was the guiding theme of my new life as the wife of a minister-in-training. Was I dressing appropriately? Acting appropriately? Speaking appropriately? I was determined I wasn't going to embarrass Luke or prove God made a mistake by entrusting His man to me. I continued my Extreme Makeover by toning down my loud-laughing, much-talking, annoying personality and adding a bit of "Christianese" to my conversations. "Dinner tonight was SUCH a BLAST!" turned into a demure "Bless you for welcoming us in your home." Not that I wasn't blessed, mind you. That just wasn't a genuine way personally for me to express it.

As time went on, I kept thinking that what I was becoming externally would somehow sink through to my heart. I'm reminded of Aaron and the priestly garments God designed for his "dignity and honor" (Ex. 28:2). The high priest's position was a dignified one, but I can't help but think how unworthy of such finery Aaron must have felt. Surely he would never forget that while Moses was communing with God and receiving instructions on how to fashion the priestly garments, he was busy fashioning a golden calf. Idol worship and three thousand dead the first time at the pulpit is not exactly the kind of beginning that inspires one to believe he is the right person for the job. I wonder how long it took before the honor of the ephod seeped into Aaron's spirit.

I'm certainly not presuming that Aaron's feelings were anything near my own, but I can tell you there is more to becoming the person you want to be than simply wearing the outfit. Putting on a Halloween mask doesn't make a person a monster any more than elastic-waist pants make a girl a preacher's wife. Despite the new outfits, I continued to struggle with feelings of inadequacy because I didn't do anything pastors' wives are typically famous for. I didn't play the piano. Didn't sing. And didn't have a signature, oft-requested food dish. It became harder and harder for me to bear the pressure this internal-external conflict demanded, so once again I found myself wondering how in the world I was supposed to "do" this preacher-wife thing, and—more important—if I even deserved such an honor.

Different Strokes

My answer came in Scripture—imagine that! Romans 12 is the chapter that first suggested to me that in the midst of transforming and renewing I could still maintain some individuality. In fact, not only does this passage suggest we embrace and find ways to express our uniqueness within Christ's church, it demands it!

The mistake I had been making all along was in believing I had to morph into a stereotype—that there was only one mold for a ministry wife and somehow I had to contort myself inside. I also believed that kind of woman was somehow on a plane above every other and must transcend the realm of a "regular" Christian. Romans 12:4–6 refutes that by stating, "For just as we have many members in one body and all the members do not have the same function, so we, who are many, are one body in Christ, and individually members of one another. Since we have gifts that differ according to the grace given to us, each of us is to exercise them accordingly" (NASB).

Gifts that differ? Differ as in *different?* Meaning I didn't have to be just like someone else? That suggestion was revolutionary to me! And God, being the One of perfect timing, allowed me to attend a ministry-wife retreat with many of the other girls from campus just as this idea was taking root in my heart. Would you like to guess what I did there? I took my first-ever, wonderfully revealing spiritual gifts test. My life would never be the same.

My test concluded I have the gifts of teaching, shepherding, and administration. All of these were a bit mysterious. I knew I loved to study God's Word but wasn't sure how that would ever translate into ministry. My Southern Baptist sensibilities made me bristle at the title of "pastor-shepherd" until I realized that simply meant loving and discipling people. Administration is laughable to me now because it implies some inherent knack for organization. Let's be clear: I love the *idea* of organization, and once upon a time I was completely uptight about schedules, a perfectly clean home, labeled containers, etc. But four kids later? Let's just say I've decided to cry uncle on that point and perhaps revisit it later in the empty-nest season of motherhood.

Assigning a title and definition to my vague, indescribable longings to serve has perhaps, short of salvation, been the single most freeing thing I've ever experienced. The realization that God created me with a unique gift in mind and that He has given me permission to exercise it accordingly has been paramount in helping me break free from the yoke I bore that required that I adhere to an unwritten set of ministry-wife standards. Jesus promised His yoke would be easy and His burden light. Your Father did not place any expectation that has you bowed over and struggling under its weight.

That doesn't mean that people won't try to bend you to their will. In the introduction, I alluded to an interesting conversation I had with a gentleman when Luke was first called to ministry. In a well-meaning way, he proceeded to advise me on how I could be the greatest asset to Luke when he began to interview with churches. To paraphrase, he told me I needed to learn to play the piano and tout my own ability to contribute in order to make Luke more "marketable."

Oh, would I have a word for anyone who shared that mentality with me today. A gracious word, but a word all the same. Back then, thankfully, I didn't have enough sense to be indignant. I wish I believed his was a rogue view, but I've encountered enough personalities since then to know that isn't the case. Unfortunately, whether the expectations placed on you are in writing or not, many parishioners have a preconceived notion of what role you are to play—especially in a more traditional church setting.

In responses to the survey on my blog regarding the pressures of ministry, I was absolutely appalled to hear that one of my sisters actually served alongside her husband in a congregation that expected her to be involved in the women's ministry board as well as to attend *every* meeting and function. They wanted to be so clear in their expectations that they wrote this into the church bylaws!

IN THE CHURCH BYLAWS! Are you kidding me?

(Pardon me while I regain my composure.)

My first reaction was not one I'd like to detail here. However, I will share my second reaction: "Well, at least they had the guts to admit on paper what many expect in principle." It's interesting to me the insanely loud ways in which people attempt to fill biblical silence.

A Word from the Word on Character Qualities

As for biblical mandates where the wife of a pastor is concerned, there are none save for the general requirements for that of a godly woman and/or helpmate (Prov. 31, Titus 2, Eph. 5, 1 Peter 3). However, there is one verse listed among the qualifications of a deacon that appears to reference his spouse. We won't debate here whether this verse is addressed to a deacon's wife or deaconess, but it stands to reason that this woman is a servant within the body and is called upon to meet certain standards. I am referring to 1 Timothy 3:11 which reads, "Even so must their wives be grave, not slanderers, sober, faithful in all things" (KJV).

I specifically chose the King James rendering of this verse because the wording is reminiscent of my own understanding of how I was supposed to act once I became the wife of a minister. The "not slan-dering" didn't seem so difficult (a view I've since recanted), but I mistakenly equated "grave" with grumpy, "sober" with reserved, and "faithful in all things" as a *doer* of all things.

I believe I've made it clear I do not believe there is a formula for transforming oneself into the perfect pastor's wife. However, after digging into this particular verse, I do believe we can draw some conclusions on what qualities will characterize a woman in servant leadership. Going one step further, in context with the location, it stands to reason that if these are characteristics a deacon's wife should meet, then they should certainly also apply to the wife of a minister. Using this verse as a guide, let's take a self-test to see how we line up with the personality Paul described. In this list, find three qualities she has and one she does not:

She is winsome.

The word *grave* used in 1 Timothy 3:11 is translated from the Greek *semnos*. Here I'll quote directly from my beloved *Hebrew-Greek Key Word Study Bible*: "Semnos does not merely indicate the earthly dignity lent to a person but is one who also owes his modesty to that higher citizenship which is also his, being one who inspires not only respect but reverence and worship. There lies something of majestic and awe-inspiring qualities in semnos *which does not repel but rather invites and attracts.*"[1]

Girls, people need to like being around you! Depending on your particular church situation, it can be very easy to cultivate a negative outlook that translates itself into the prune-faced preacher's wife some people have come to expect. At times, the cause is pressure from within the body. Conflict, especially if directed toward her husband, can tempt a girl to withdraw affection from the entire crowd. At other times, our own sinful piety is the wedge Satan uses to fracture our relationships within the church. I can't tell you the number of times I have repented for bitterness toward individuals who complain about our ministries and yet never darken the doors outside of Sunday mornings. Instead of serving with gladness, I gripe and grumble when things are undone or when my hubby literally has to beg from the pulpit to get people to fill positions.

If we aren't careful, the negative aspects of ministry can quickly overshadow the wonderful, positive things that God is doing in our midst. When we give our minds over to depressing, destructive thoughts, we will naturally become unpleasant company. Your husband needs you to be the beating heart behind his ministry! There have been so many church members I've known who liked their pastor but would quickly tell you his wife was his warmth and personality. People are much more likely to overlook faults when mutual love undergirds the relationship. And, in order for people to love you, you need to present yourself as lovable. First Peter 4:7–8 tells us, "The end of all things is near. Therefore be clear minded and self-controlled so that you can pray. Above all, love each other deeply, because love covers over a multitude of sins." (I should also mention the next verse talks about not grumbling.)

So why is this important? There is definitely benefit for your family when your congregation is endeared to you personally through your charming personality. However, the relationship we desire to build even more is that between the parishioners and God.

Remember the rest of the *semnos* definition? When we can owe our attitudes to the empowerment of the Holy Spirit, we inspire not only respect for ourselves but also worship and reverence for Him. There is nothing about my stinky attitude that leads others to be more devoted to Christ. But if I react graciously when there is no earthly reason why I should? He will get the glory for that, my friends. Try it for yourself and watch it work.

She is sober.

This word isn't talking about drunkenness though I do hope that is a given. In this context, *sober* is defined as "to be calm and collected in spirit."[2]

There are a couple of things about this particular word that helped clear up a personal misconception in one area but also gave me fair warning in another.

I mentioned earlier that I am a bit of a loudmouth. Maybe I didn't quite say it in that way, but it is definitely what I meant. One thing I thought I would have to learn to do as a pastor's wife was sit quietly with my hands folded—yet one more problem for me because I talk with my hands, too. The true definition of *sober* was a huge comfort because it helped me understand that God called not only *us* but our *personalities* as well as an aid to our husbands' ministries. I think there is a vast difference between being calm and collected in spirit versus being calm and collected in demeanor. Do you love to laugh? Giggle your head off! Are you quiet by nature? Then be composed. What your people and your God want from you is authenticity. They both know if you are faking it. It takes way too much effort to operate against your wiring. You'll only end up burned-out and bitter.

In understanding the importance of embracing one's own personality and giftedness, I have particularly benefited from the testimony of Lois Evans (wife of Oak Cliff Bible Church's pastor, Dr. Tony Evans). She is quick to credit her husband with giving her the freedom to express herself within the body of Christ. Mrs. Evans shares openly about the anxieties she faced in her beginning years of being the wife of a senior pastor, a position she told God she never wanted. There came a point when Tony set her free by telling her he only wanted her to be herself. "I don't know why that was such a big deal," she says, "but it brought me to a reality that yes, God created me to be me, and even before He placed me in my mother's womb, He had a plan for my life."[3] I am so grateful to have a husband who also has given his blessing for me to be a sanctified version of the girl he married—loud mouth and all. I can honestly say we are each other's biggest cheerleader. Any real or perceived expectations I felt to be anything more or different never came from him. I have talked with many, many ministry wives on this particular subject. Every single one of them has shared that her husband's support and encouragement was paramount in her feeling the freedom to be true to her calling and personality.

In addition to being calm and collected, there is further implication of sobriety. The word also means "to be circumspect or heedful of circumstances and potential consequences; prudent."[4]

Here is where we can all use a good warning: A woman of sobriety is a woman of pause. She thinks before she acts. She prays before she speaks. This is calm and collected in action. Let me give you an example.

I just received an email three minutes ago that I suppose God meant for an illustration of this very point. Without divulging details, my first instinct is to close this document immediately and fire off a response that will put this girl in her place. She is wrong, she is causing problems, and she has hurt my friend. However, I pause.

What in a hasty, irritable response will cause this woman to be more devoted to God? What words of mine will prick her conscience for what she has done? This is a situation where only God's Word will speak. If I don't take the time to pray for the proper response, to search out the timely Scripture, and most important, to extend grace, then ultimately I've done nothing but turn her heart away from me and away from the God I profess in front of her daily. I'm so glad I was working on this paragraph right now. This could have gotten ugly.

She is faithful.

The Greek word for "faithful" used in this verse is *pistos*. In short, it refers to one who can be relied upon.[5] As I type this sentence I cringe over how many times I have said yes first and asked questions later. Of how many times I've overextended myself for the sake of doing what I said I would do even when I begrudged every second of it. Of times when I've done ten things halfway instead of one thing well.

Faithfulness ties intimately to the two previous characteristics listed. When we are comfortable in our skin and secure in our calling then it is much easier to give out our yes with confidence without fearing the criticism of those who think we should be doing more. It is also incredibly important to note that the life season you are currently in will dictate how much you are able to contribute to the ministries of the church.

I've known many women who grieved the enforced solitude that often comes with raising young children. I have to be honest and say there have been times when I've thought I could have so much more kingdom effectiveness if I weren't tied to changing diapers and the other never-ending duties that accompany motherhood.

As recently as two weeks ago, this very point burned my britches. In planning for a summer mission trip our church takes each year, Luke suggested we bring the children along. I fired off, "Well, if you are going to do that, I'll just stay home because there is no way I'll get anything accomplished if I'm taking care of four kids." Mature response, huh?

At the time I made this statement, we were with some dear friends, Jeff and Kelly, who also serve in ministry. Kelly gently encouraged me by sharing how taking her own children on the same trip the year before had changed their lives and had set their hearts ablaze in compassion for others. That year, her mission ministry was to her children. Her testimony reminded me it doesn't matter how reliable I am outside my home if I've not faithfully ministered within it.

So guess who's going on the mission trip?

Now that we have considered the three things a ministry wife should be, let's look at one thing she shouldn't.

She isn't *diabolical.*

I mentioned earlier that not being a slanderer seemed like the easiest one of this list of requirements. You may or may not be aware that the Greek word for slander is *diabolos*. We get our English word *diabolical* from this root, but there is another translation that is even more interesting: *Diabolos* is the Greek word for the Devil. It literally means "one who falsely accuses and divides people without any reason. He is an accuser, a slanderer. Satan is called by that name because originally he accused or slandered God in paradise."[6]

None of us wants to admit to ever having been someone's Satan, but we've all been guilty in one way or another. All of us have to admit that confidences have been broken, unfair assumptions made, and accusations launched. I've known this to happen accidentally, but I'm also aware of situations where a ministry wife used her knowledge and influence to intentionally destroy another's credibility. Most of the time, the root motivation was to be sure she and her husband were perceived as "right" no matter the cost or casualties left behind.

Unfortunately, there are those not spiritually mature enough to cope with great amounts of information. Let's face it, who doesn't like to feel they are "in the know"? Who isn't tempted to add their two cents to a conversation centered on the latest church conflict? When I was younger in ministry, I have to admit that I pumped Luke for details under the guise of wanting to know "how to pray." (He always saw through that one. Ha!) The truth is I just wanted to satisfy my own curiosity.

I can tell you now that the less I know the better I like it. As if I need anything else to tax my mind? Luke doesn't share sensitive information with me not because he doesn't trust me with it but because he doesn't want me to bear the burden of knowing what he has to deal with. There are counseling situations that could potentially cause me to look at people differently even though I wouldn't want to. Luke is the shepherd of his flock and the caretaker of our home, and if he tells me I don't want to know, I trust him. I have no problem being blissfully ignorant.

Many of my ministry-wife friends tell me the one thing they wish the congregation knew is that their husband doesn't tell them everything. I can certainly amen that! This isn't only limited to sensitive information but to general information as well. I tell people all the time that if they want me specifically to know something then they will have to tell me face-to-face. It can be a source of aggravation when we are expected to act on information we do not have!

The Bottom Line

I've said time and time again that there is no formula for becoming the perfect pastor's wife, but the Bible is full of wisdom on how to become more like Christ. The qualities we've just discussed are a tiny piece of what a life sanctified to service will look like.

I am reminded of Psalm 15:1–4, which reads,

> LORD, who may dwell in your sanctuary?
>   Who may live on your holy hill?
> He whose walk is blameless
>   and who does what is righteous,
> who speaks the truth from his heart
>   and has no slander on his tongue,
> who does his neighbor no wrong
>   and casts no slur on his fellowman,

who despises a vile man
    but honors those who fear the Lord,
who keeps his oath
    even when it hurts.

You'll notice that every trait listed has nothing to do with a woman meeting expectations of those around her but rather with one who aspires to be worthy to dwell in the sanctuary of God. Our righteous confidence comes from identification with His Son. As for me, I no longer feel the need to borrow clothes from my grandmother's closet. I love my huge sunglasses. I'm crazy about my boot-cut jeans that *do not* have an elastic waist. But more than anything, I love the God dwelling in me who has given me permission to walk authentically before Him and His people.

And to add blessing on top of blessing, I believe He's completely okay with the fact I'm walking in a great pair of heels.

Round Table

Believe it or not, the issue of clothing and other externals are the ones I am asked about most often. Hello? M2M Girls? Let's hear what you think!

- "As I was growing up, my pastor's wife was perfect. She was beautiful, could sing, and could teach a women's group or Sunday school class with a smile and never break a sweat. I, however, came from the 'grunge' generation. So when I met my husband—knowing that he wanted to be a pastor—I was hesitant to embrace the role of pastor's wife. It took me a while to realize that God did not want me to try to be someone else or try to live up to imaginary expectations from those in the church, but He also did not want me to stay the same. I guess I am still learning daily, but I love to look back and see what God has done in my life in the last thirteen years."—Call Me Mara (name withheld)

- "I think it is important to be who we are in Christ; then we will be genuine and real in our daily relationships. If I am insecure in my position in Christ, then there will be too much focus on what others think of me. I passionately believe that ALL Christian women should aim to be more like Christ—not just the pastor's wife. If my life and marriage can be a window to help spur other women toward Christ, then 'bring it on'!"—Elisarose @ Lizzy's Busies

- "When we first entered the ministry, I did feel the need to be as perfect as possible in everything I did, but I soon learned that made some people (women mostly) feel uncomfortable and inadequate. Being myself and allowing others to do the same and loving them unconditionally has been very successful for me."—Sherry @ Life at the Parsonage

- "I have found that the congregation, mainly the women, want me to be like them—not pious, more holy, just me! They want me to have a spiritual side so that they can come to me in times of need, but they also want me to have a fun-loving, normal side so that we can be friends."—Julie

- "When God called my husband into ministry full-time, He also put a burden and a call on my heart. I had someone ask me, 'So what are you going to do differently now that you will be a pastor's wife?' I thought about it and was disturbed at first to think that I had to be 'different' now. But God spoke to my spirit and said, 'Just love the people, and I will do the rest.' So that is what I have done, and God has given me the wisdom, the grace, and the love for ministry that I share with my husband."—Laurie @ Women Taking a Stand

- "I would like for pastors' wives to know I pray sincerely for them. I'm sure it is tough when you feel like you can't be completely open with someone for fear of what they might think of you and then they judge your husband based on your words or actions."—Be Present, Be Real (layperson, name withheld)

- "In days gone by I think the pastor's wife was expected to fill a lot of shoes. Today I don't think it is as much. I'm sure there are still those who feel they need to be everything, but it's not like that at my church. Our pastor's wife is a wonderful woman with a heart for prayer and an awesome artist! She serves God tremendously in those areas."—Kim @ A Stone Gatherer (layperson)

Now That You Know:

1. What kind of identity crisis have you experienced? How did you resolve it? (If you haven't, I hope this chapter helped you begin!)

2. Has your hubby gone out of his way to reassure you that he has no expectations for you other than to be yourself? Make an effort to do that same thing for him. If you've not yet had this conversation, now is a great time to establish open communication about the support you need from each other. Unity will make it much easier to fend off criticism from others.

3. Laypeople: Nothing makes me feel better than when people go out of their way to acknowledge something unique they feel I contribute to Luke's ministry and/or the church. Do the same for your ministry wife. A few encouraging words will make her week!

Three

I CAN POTENTIALLY BE MY HUSBAND'S WORST ENEMY

Submission is knowing how to duck
so God can hit your husband.
—Dr. Tony Evans

Sundays are challenging in the McKay home. And you know what? I really do try to avoid that! I've bathed the kids and gotten our clothes ready the night before. I've risen early and said my prayers in an attempt to retain my composure. I've played our favorite praise music to focus our minds on worship. Even with all that, I'm ashamed to say the hushed tones of my supplication are often replaced with shouts of, "Would you kids *please* brush your teeth and quit wrinkling your shirt and stop touching each other and finish eating your breakfast and find your other shoe before we are late?! AGAIN!"

And then there is Luke. I'm not certain when the Sunday Morning Meetings began or even if there really is such a thing. All I know is these "meetings" seem to get earlier and earlier, leaving me home alone to get four children under the age of twelve to church on time. In my estimation, that's not an ideal setup to prepare a mom's heart for an encounter with God. Or perhaps it's the perfect way. Who needs Him more than a woman in the full throes of a meltdown?

I remember one morning when I'd had enough. Luke came in to tell me that, yet again, he had to leave early to get to church. I went berserk! "It must be nice being you!" I yelled. Needless to say, the fight was on. Both of us were determined to garner the most sympathy. We stomped into separate rooms, convinced neither had any support from the other. God must have been incredibly proud.

It didn't take but a few minutes for my guilty conscience to kick in. All I could think about was the fact I'd sent God's man-of-the-hour (as the pastor is often called here in the southern United States) off to church not with a kiss on the cheek but a punch to the heart. I'd been his personal Satan that morning and I was ashamed. (*Diabolical, I must not be diabolical!*) Clearly it was time for a shift in perspective.

I asked God to help me with my terrible attitude, and He immediately brought to mind the plight of single moms. I have undying admiration for these dear women who get the kids off to daycare/school and still manage somehow to get to work on time. I pout and complain over having to get the family somewhere by ten one day per week (only yards away from the house, I might add), and they do it five days a week, sometimes more, with no relief in sight. Now when I feel tempted to sink back into my woe-is-me ways, it is a reminder to pray for single mothers whose circumstances are much more stressful than my own. I also learned to comfort myself with the thought, "I'll have Luke back on Monday."

Considering this, I asked some of our buddies in the congregation to hold me accountable to this somewhat tongue-in-cheek pledge:

> *I hereby declare I will not give Luke any grief from*
> *sunup to sundown on the Lord's Day. As long as there*
> *is light in the sky, all he'll get from me is a Sunday*
> *Sundae made of a "Yes, dear" with a smile on top.* *

> *(*Come sundown all bets are off.)*

Though at first meant to be a joke, this little creed has made all the difference in the attitude I have toward supporting my husband in his calling instead of nursing my own sense of entitlement— especially on the day he needs to be encouraged above all others. (I should mention that the nicer I am, the later those mysterious morning meetings are scheduled to begin. Do you think the two are related?)

Our willingness to lay our own comforts aside is just one way we can give our men the freedom needed to go storm the gates of hell. However, if the two of you are already in that battle within your home, there isn't much energy left to crusade for the kingdom. Satan knows this and will come after your families fully loaded to make sure you never make it out the front door with any semblance of healthy ministry. That is why we have to learn to recognize what's in the belly of the Trojan horses he sends our way so we can best defend one of the most precious gifts of God—our marriage.

The Necessity of a Healthy Marriage

In a presentation to the 2008 Southern Baptist Pastor's Conference held in San Antonio, Texas, Dr. Gary Chapman stated, "Pastors and their wives not only have a responsibility to minister, but also a duty to exemplify the way Christ commands marriages to be."[1]

That single sentence challenges and scares me to death at the same time. It's a huge deal that people look to our relationship as a model for their own. In this same speech, Dr. Chapman also predicted that "when ministry marriage begins exemplifying the biblical model, non-Christians will flock to the church for answers to their own marital struggles."[2] The responsibility of modeling Christ's love for the church should be all the motivation we need to shore up any shaky walls in our relationships.

The Gold Standard

Any person looking for the scriptural ideal for marriage will not have to search long before landing in Ephesians 5:22–33. In verse 32, Paul calls the parallel of Christ's love for the church and a man's love and union with his wife "a profound mystery." The Greek word for "mystery" is *musterion* and denotes "a spiritual truth couched under an external representation or similitude, and concealed or hidden thereby unless some explanation be given."[3] According to this definition, Christ demonstrates His great love for the church by employing the picture of our marriage relationships. Though all Christians are called to this ideal, how much more relevant is this text for ministry families since the church is interwoven throughout the instructions? Let's consider this passage a bit more to see how it applies.

The S-Word

I shudder to think how many different ways the verse, "Wives, submit to your husbands as to the Lord" (Eph. 5:22), has been misinterpreted. Forget about the sin of unbelievers—I'm concerned about churchgoing men who have touted this principle as a justification in browbeating and otherwise degrading their wives in the name of Christianity.

I wish I could say this behavior was limited to laypeople mistaken in their interpretation of Scripture on the issue. Unfortunately, I've witnessed too many examples of overbearing pastors who oppress their wives and children. It is difficult to pinpoint exact statistics because very little research has been done on the issue, but according to the research conducted by the Christian Coalition Against Domestic Abuse (CCADA), "Religion is NOT a deterrent.... [T]here is just as much abuse (spousal, child, and sexual) in Christian homes as in non-Christian homes. In addition, spiritual abuse is always a component of abusive behaviors and damages the abused person's view of God."[4]

The founder of CCADA knows this heartache firsthand. Her name is Kate Johnson, and she was a battered minister's wife. I had the opportunity to converse with Kate, and her account of physical and mental abuse at the hand of her minister husband chilled me to the bone. Adding insult to injury, this man is still in ministry because the leadership would not act on his problem. Thankfully, Kate is in a much better place today, and out of her pain her own ministry was born. Through her organization, she seeks to give counsel to women who find themselves in this desperate situation.

Now obviously this is a deep ocean of a topic and not one into which I'm prepared to dive for our purposes. However, in context with the passage we are examining, it is necessary to talk about what submission is and what it is not. The mutual yielding of a husband and wife to one another as described in Ephesians 5 is a beautiful thing and looks nothing like the ugly instance I just gave you. I implore you, if you are or know someone in this situation, please begin by contacting CCADA (see Resources for information) for godly guidance.

Mutual Empowerment

Many books have been written on the topic of biblical manhood and womanhood, but my absolute favorite is *What's the Difference? Manhood and Womanhood Defined According to the Bible* by John Piper. (Of course, a lot of my absolute favorite books are by Piper, but that's an obsession that needs to be dealt with elsewhere!) In this fabulous little manual, Piper gives two definitions of what a man and woman operating under God's ideal will look like:

1. At the heart of mature masculinity is a sense of benevolent responsibility to lead, provide for, and protect women in ways appropriate to a man's differing relationships.

2. At the heart of mature femininity is a freeing disposition to affirm, receive, and nurture strength and leadership from worthy men in ways appropriate to a woman's differing relationships.[5]

Allow me to give you a visual on a woman empowering her man to his good and her gain. Suppose there is a man who suffers an accident that confines him to a wheelchair. His limited mobility has made it impossible for him to do many of the chores around the home in which he previously took pride. His recovery period will be long—if there is a recovery at all.

This man's wife is heartbroken over the emotional effects he is experiencing from being unable to complete even the menial job of mowing the lawn. She gets an idea. What if she can create a way he can help? She wheels her husband into the yard, puts a weed whacker into his hands, and gives him the task of trimming while she cuts grass.

It would have been much easier for her to leave her hubby inside watching television while she took control and did the "man chores" that he couldn't. However, submission chooses the harder yet more honorable thing. She places herself under her infirmed husband even though it makes perfect sense for her to take the lead, and she gives him dignity and respect by providing the tools he needs to exercise his manhood—not working circles around him even though she could. And because he is aware of her sacrifice, he cherishes her all the more. The resulting adoration is what I believe the apostle Paul had in mind when he penned Ephesians 5:25: "Husbands, love your wives, just as Christ loved the church and gave himself up for her."

Balancing the Give-and-Take

Ephesians 5:33 reads, "However, each one of you also must love his wife as he loves himself, and the wife must respect her husband." This verse gives an excellent wrap-up on the reciprocal nature of marriage. Every religious and secular book I've read on marriage typically agrees a man's number one need is respect while the woman's is love. Paul didn't need a master's degree in counseling to come to this same conclusion. If a man loves his wife as himself, he'll get the respect he desires. If a woman respects her man, she'll be showered with the affection on which she was created to thrive. Submission is not a one-sided event in which the woman is forced to relinquish her power (as the feminist movement would have us believe) but rather a dance of give-and-take where both the man and woman love in the best interest of the other.

So now I have but one question for you: Referring to Piper's definitions of manhood and womanhood, what maturely feminine woman would have any problem nestling herself in the arms of care and provision that a maturely masculine man longs to wrap around her? Seriously, why would you want to rob yourself of that? The answer is … YOU WOULDN'T! Respect your man's role as the head of your home and church even if it would make sense sometimes to do otherwise. Receive your hubby's protection and wisdom as a gift. It's one that will keep on giving—if you let it.

Why does all of this matter? Because your marriage role-plays the mystery of the Great Dance between Christ and His beloved bride, the church. The bond the congregation perceives you have with your man and the submission you have to one another will color every area of his ministry and will be either a great help or a hindrance in God's using your family to counsel others in distress.

Let's Get Practical

As in all the other chapters, I conducted a survey on my blog asking women about specific pitfalls of ministry that, if left unchecked, could put a strain on their marriage. Before we talk about those, allow me a disclaimer.

Many of the responders accurately and wisely stated that ministry itself isn't the source of strife and that the simple act of sharing the love of Christ does not strain a marriage. However, when our personal devotion time is suffering, when our boundaries are blurred, and when Satan creeps in, sowing seeds of bitterness and discontent, it is only a matter of time before a blowup. So please keep this in mind as I continue by talking about issues prevalent in ministry that, coupled with these other deficiencies, can be of great detriment to our marital relationships.

The Dreaded Phone

I join my sisters in the belief that the telephone is the most devious device in Satan's arsenal. Talk about a Trojan horse! This little gadget (with numbers published in the Sunday bulletin) disguises itself as a symbol of our hubby's availability to his flock, and yet call after call flows out of it well into the night for matters that are less than an emergency.

My friend and fellow pastor's wife Kelli cracked me up by telling me her family has a Bat Phone. I think many of us have a Bruce Wayne who is convinced the world will explode if he doesn't answer. This is one area where my hubby and I are polar opposites. I personally believe voice mail is Jesus' deliverance from Hotline Bondage, but Luke doesn't quite agree. He thinks I am causing myself extra work by having to call someone back instead of answering right away.

Who said I was going to call back? (Just kidding. Sort of.)

Now obviously the size and mentality of your church is a huge factor in dictating how serious an issue this can become. I had an interesting email exchange about this very subject with a pastor's wife who was adamant that no minister should be taking phone calls from the congregation while at home—urgency being no exception. "That's what deacons and elders are for," she said.

In a perfect world, she is absolutely right. I realize many of you serve in larger churches with pastoral care staff or a team of people to deal with needs of the parishioners. Some congregations have well-organized deacon ministries where each servant is assigned a portion of the population to tend to their needs. The reality for the smaller church (the majority of congregations) is that the pastor is often the only staff and the deacons and elders are not willing or able to serve in this capacity. Is this the New Testament model? No. But can the pastor change without backlash what has been a long-standing tradition? Not overnight.

The whole issue of the biblical role of deacons is not one I care to address. But I can tell you that in the traditional church a pastor who begins expecting a previously inactive group of men to start visiting members of the body and protecting his time for study of the Word will quickly be met with the "But that's what we pay you for" attitude. The question a pastor begins asking himself is, "Isn't it just easier to make the call or visit myself than be disappointed when no one agrees to help—or worse, have people think I'm not doing my job?" I know for us, right or wrong, the answer has been yes. For that reason, we've had to come up with creative ways to deal with the reality instead of ranting about how we shouldn't have to.

I don't want to make it sound as if we have no boundaries, because we definitely qualify which situations warrant being absent from the family either in mind or body. Keep in mind, though, it is sometimes our husband's own self-imposed expectations and not the lack of help from leadership that keep him working overtime. Only you and your husband can determine where to draw your personal line and agree to always step back when one of you feels it's being crossed.

Many women in the survey responded that their husbands' unrestrained use of the phone, email, instant messaging, and texting communicated to them that the needs of the church people were more important than those at home. It is best to talk about these feelings sooner rather than later. I truly believe that no husband ever sets about to neglect his family, but uncontrolled time on the phone while home with the family is often the first step down a slippery slope.

The Invisible Husband

I received an email from a senior pastor's wife once that said, "My husband is a great minister to everyone but me." I've said before and don't plan on stopping now: There is no such thing as "successful" ministry if the home is in shambles. First Samuel 16:7 reminds us, "The Lord does not look at the things man looks at. Man looks at the outward appearance, but the Lord looks at the heart."

I believe the same concept is at work in our public ministries versus our private lives. Often we can be so caught up in making sure our churches are deemed a success that we forget to exert the same amount of effort in our husband-wife relationship. When the resulting problems become too obvious to ignore, the temptation is to conceal the rift so our congregations remain unaware of any problems in our home. It should come as no surprise that God is not interested in appearances. He wants consistency and transparency. That doesn't mean we are expected to be faultless, but we are obligated to make a wholehearted attempt to practice what we preach.

It is my belief that men who have deluded themselves by thinking God will provide for their families while they are out ministering have grossly misunderstood the qualifications of the office. Sadly, pastoral neglect is a rarely addressed subject. Because of this, many a woman has become embittered against her husband and her God, whom she perceives is the reason for her husband's absence.

There are many different ways a wife can feel unimportant, but most are seated in the belief the church has taken first place in priority over the family. It is a truly foolish man who believes he's doing heaven a favor by abandoning his family on a regular basis.

This is one area where I've been supremely blessed because I do not doubt that Luke always wants to be with our family first. But that doesn't mean there haven't been seasons or instances when I felt he left the best of himself at the church.

Financial Pressures

Please tell me if I'm wrong, but the majority of our husbands did not enter ministry on the promise of a fat paycheck. In a 2001 study, the Barna Research Group concluded,

> *Clergy compensation is especially noteworthy because more than two-thirds of all Senior Pastors have a graduate-level degree. Other professionals with that level of education earn average salaries over $60,000 or more, depending upon their profession. Many church-goers, however, expect their pastor to earn less than the national average because they are involved in ministry, regardless of their school loans and family obligations. Pastors who have a seminary degree receive an average compensation package of $42,083—significantly above the average for pastors without a seminary degree ($31,500), but notably below the national norm for professionals with advanced degrees.*[6]

Honey, it doesn't look like we'll be taking that vacation to Hawaii after all.

Money, and specifically lack of it, can strain any marriage. According to financial counselor Dave Ramsey, "Money is the No.

1 cause of divorce—not to mention the thing married couples fight about most."[7] Considering the reality that ministry is traditionally an underpaid position, it's no surprise this can be a huge source of stress.

Luke and I still experience this same pressure but dealt with it even more so when he was new in ministry and bivocational. With four young children, having a traditional punch-the-clock job wasn't a viable option for me since child care would quickly eat away any money I could make. I also felt a personal conviction to be a full-time mom. So we asked God to help us in this area, and He orchestrated a job I could do on a flexible schedule: cleaning offices. Yes, girls. I was a cleaning lady—and proud of it!

I have many girlfriends who have chosen creative ways to earn money from home. For a period of time, God grew my cleaning business to a size that I needed employees. I was thrilled there was no shortage of stay-at-home moms willing to fill those positions. Some women sell homemade items (hair bows, specialty baby products, etc.) on eBay or Etsy.com. Others are home-party hosts (Pampered Chef, Avon, Mary Kay, Princess House, etc.). Established bloggers can also monetize their Web sites, though this type of income isn't something you can expect overnight. I've been blogging for two years and so far have gotten only a pen engraved with my name and a few free books, so don't count on it to make the house payment.

The point is, God knows your needs, and if it includes extra income from your doing some type of work, I believe He will give you the desire and energy to do what is needed. One of my favorite sayings is, "You do what you have to do!" I look back now on the years Luke and I took turns cleaning office buildings in the wee hours of the night and wonder how in the world we survived. Now I realize God gave us the stamina to do what was necessary to make it. I commend ministry wives who work full-time jobs outside the home to contribute to the family money bag. Often, a minister would be unable to continue in the calling without the financial support his wife provides.

Unfortunately, many ministry families get themselves into terrible financial situations when they begin depending on credit cards and loans to subsidize their income. Take it from someone who has walked this road in seminary: Just say no! It is so tempting to swipe the card when there is no money for groceries or the doctor bills are due. But credit is only a temporary fix and, just like any snare of Satan, it will cost far more than you were ever willing to pay. Nipping credit card usage in the bud will cause you less pain now than later. If you are in this mess now, pray, pray, pray that God will show you how to steward your current finances or provide work to make up the difference. He will be faithful! Most important, keep a positive, open line of communication with your husband on the matter or this can quickly become a marriage and ministry destroyer.

Moral Breakdown

There is no ministry immune to the possibility of moral failure. This can come in the form of physical abuse, drug and substance abuse, and marital unfaithfulness. However, one problem is quickly blowing away the statistics among ministers: pornography.

I am privileged to know a minister's wife by the name of Cindy Beall. She and her husband, Chris, candidly share the story of his pornography addiction and extramarital affairs in her ebook, *Life After Porn.* (Find the full story at CindyBeall.com.) Cindy's story—from the heartbreaking account of the day her husband confessed his sin to the victory God has given her family through his recovery—is one that puts a face on this disturbing blight on our families.

Though the reasons for this behavior run deep and are difficult to understand at best, there is an interesting common explanation ministers give for why they first engaged in pornography. One man in a television interview explained, "[Pornography] was one place I could turn where I could be the one receiving instead of giving." That comment unnerved me until I took a moment to consider what he was really saying. Though obviously I don't agree with the outlet he used to deal with his stress, I can be cautiously compassionate toward the despair that caused him to arrive at that place.

When I read this last paragraph to Luke he said, "Do you agree with what that guy said?" Absolutely not! One of the chief lies of Satan is to have us believe we have needs that God cannot meet. Sin occurs when we choose another path to self-gratification. Explaining away why we sinned means nothing—eventually the finger has to point back at our own selfishness.

With that said, I would not dare presume to give dos and don'ts on "porn-proofing" your marriage because I in no way believe a wife is responsible if her husband is ensnared. What I will tell you is to learn to recognize when conditions are ripe for it to be a temptation. Is your husband overly stressed? Is there strife in your marriage?

Has your husband ever admitted lust is an area of weakness for him? These are just a few questions you and he can consider together now instead of later that will help guard your marriage from this life- and ministry-shattering transgression.

The Other Women

I don't like to describe myself as the jealous type, but the reality is, I'm the jealous type. My pet joke with Luke is to tell him he is hot under the collar. (Get it? Some ministers wear a collar? He's good-looking?) Oh well, I can say that because he's my husband and I like to believe we can be playful with one another whether we are forty or eighty. With that said, Luke is one handsome guy, and any woman who tries to put her paws on my husband had better be ready for a catfight.

Many of your congregations have a Ms. Touchy-Feely. She's the one who is always trying to get a full-on pastor hug. Who always needs counseling. Who never comes close to your husband if you are near.

Luke and I have encountered these types before, and I'm sure we will again. Having a plan for dealing with the association with and counseling of women will ensure you will not be caught off guard. Here are just a few things we do:

Run a block for him during entrance/dismissal from services. In one of our pastorates, a woman who loved to wallow on Luke used arrival and dismissal as her opportunity for an attempted hug from the preacher. She made him terribly uncomfortable and me just downright mad. I stayed close to him before and after services to run interference. I finally gave enough woman signals (you know the unspoken body language just short of dirty looks I'm talking about) for her to know I was on to her game, so she eventually gave up. Good thing for her.

Be prepared to join in counseling sessions. Luke never, ever, never counsels a woman alone. When a woman requests counseling, he immediately stipulates I must be present in the room. If she says no, he says no. Simple as that. A woman in dire circumstances does not need any reason to look at the minister as her confidant, protector, or problem solver. Your being present states clearly he is not available for anything other than biblical advice.

Feed marital friendship. I talk to Luke often while he's away from the house. Please understand it isn't out of a sense of distrust but rather a by-product of the close relationship we have. The poor guy couldn't have a girlfriend if he wanted one because I'd interrupt their date at least half a dozen times with requests to bring home a gallon of milk or to pick up one of our kids. Notice I said, "*If* he wanted one." I don't take for granted that I need to make sure he doesn't! I hope you understand my meaning when I say if we aren't fun to be around, some other woman will gladly step in. I work hard at cultivating the friendship aspect of our marriage. Believe it or not, I'd rather talk to Luke on the phone more than any girlfriend I have. He makes me laugh my head off! I want to be the same kind of friend to him. Going back to the issue of being winsome in chapter 2—this characteristic is perhaps most important when directed toward your man. He needs to look forward to talking with you every day instead of bracing himself for a bad attitude.

Round Table

The M2M Girls couldn't quit talking about this one. Here's what they had to say when asked about potential marriage pitfalls:

- "What peeves me most is the phone. While my husband is home in body, he is on the phone. I wish I could just get him to cut it off."—Cassandra @ Tripping Around the Sun

- "There has only been one pastor's wife I've known who seemed to be more of a hindrance than a help in her husband's ministry. She was trying to 'wear the pants' in both the home and the church. It left her husband looking weak and ineffective."—Bethany (layperson) @ Beyond This Moment

- "Our marriage nearly fell apart three months after we left ministry. There were numerous reasons, but the main one was lack of intimacy. We had protected ourselves from getting too close to church members for so long we had forgotten how to connect with one another and didn't even know it."—Kristen @ We Are THAT Family

- "I think being in the ministry together has actually made our marriage and our love for each other much stronger than if we didn't have such a compelling common mission. If that weren't the case, I could see how ministry could cause some major problems—just like any time the husband and wife are not united."—Bethany @ My Life in Black and White

- "We had an experience where our pastor had an affair with a college student. None of the congregation knew this. Truth is, his wife didn't even know about it. So, in effect, our church walked around the problem and did nothing to help this marriage, which then dissolved."—Holly (layperson) @ Crown Laid Down

- "Limited income is definitely not the best aspect of ministry. My sister and her husband both work and are looking for a new house. I have times of jealousy because I want a big house and the nicest things too. But we are the recipients of many blessings because people know of our limited income."—Julie @ Sisters

- "I have learned to give my husband his space before he preaches and not be argumentative or burden him with any unnecessary news until after church. I have to remember if I don't embrace his calling and support him, I will be held accountable. A woman can make or break her man's ministry."—Kelli @ Ponderings of a Pastor's Wife

- "We have three small children, and I really have to try hard not to resent him for not being able to help me get them up, fed, and dressed, and to church on Sunday mornings. I have to remind myself a LOT that Sunday is a workday for him and I need to just grin and bear it."—Leigh Ann @ The Jones Family

- "I have gotten jealous over my husband's time and energy. As preschool pastor, he works with many women. He has never given me a reason to be jealous. This is all between Satan and me, but it has helped me realize the importance of boundaries when you work with the opposite sex. I am also very involved and present in his ministry, and I know the ladies well."—Erin @ Chad's Girls

Now That You Know:

1. When is the last time you and your husband were intentional about spending quality time together? How has either of you gone out of your way in the past to plan a surprise outing? This doesn't have to be expensive. Take a walk. Go to your favorite restaurant for lunch. Visit a flea market.

2. Constantly evaluate the health of your marriage. Don't let bitterness take root! If you feel your husband is neglecting the family, tell him gently and give him space and time to do something about it.

3. Above all else, pray for your husband, your marriage, and your ministry. Set up a private email account for him and send him special prayers and Scripture to encourage him.

4. Laypeople: Do you ever sense your ministry family is in need of a break? Arrange a night out with babysitting if needed. Send them to a great conference you know they would both enjoy. The profit from this investment will far outweigh the cost.

Four

CHURCH CAN HURT

Difficulty is behind, fear is before, though
he's got on The Hill, the Lions roar. A
Christian man is never long at ease: when
one fright's gone, another doth him seize.
—*John Bunyan,* The Pilgrim's Progress

I'll never forget the first time church broke my heart.

After Luke's graduation from Bible college, we were serving as volunteer staff in our home church as we sought God's will for our continued ministry. High on zeal but low on experience, we never saw it coming when the pastor we were serving under began feeling threatened by the affection of the congregation toward Luke. They had been present at his birth, prayed through his years of rebellion, and were overjoyed at the fact their prodigal had returned home—as a minister no less! The current pastor was relatively new, so there was no personal history to assure him we would never usurp his authority or covet his position as shepherd of this flock.

The situation deteriorated when a suggestion was made in a business meeting (which we did not attend) that Luke be called as associate pastor. We were told the church wanted this but didn't know the idea violated pulpit politics since it did not originate with the pastor. We didn't know it would seal his distrust of us. We didn't know it would result in the only total fallout we've ever experienced with a church leader. We didn't know a mind-boggling, nothing-further-from-the-truth accusation would find us crying our eyes out and literally fleeing through the back door of our beloved church, never to return.

We just didn't know.

I can safely say the entire experience shattered me to the core. How can church people—like-minded, Christ-loving people—cut each other to shreds? How can love and trust turn to bitterness and suspicion seemingly overnight? These may seem like naive questions, but I suspect they are common. There are some realities in life that are never meant to be digested, and dissension in the body of Christ is certainly one of them.

As much as the controversy Luke and I faced flabbergasted me, catching me even more off guard were the evil thoughts that rose in me during this ordeal. No one told me to expect such intense protectiveness when people were critical of my husband. I didn't know I could muster such bitterness toward another individual. I have forgiven and have been forgiven much for my behavior, but at that time and in several since I seriously could have physically injured a person or two. Okay, not really. But only because I've heard hitting people hurts, and I'm not a huge fan of pain.

In the surveys I conducted on my blog, women overwhelmingly told me the most difficult part of ministry is being cordial to someone who has attacked her husband or family. I wholeheartedly respond with an "amen, sister!" I suspect many of you have your own tales of woe where relationships within the body are concerned. Criticism and subsequent conflict can come from misunderstanding of our intent and vision. Tradition also places a huge burden on ministry couples to conform to a set of unwritten standards that everyone apparently knows but us. Denominational policies may also place you in a church where there is inherited conflict predating the apostles.

Diverging opinions are inevitable wherever more than one person gathers. It is a healthy environment where all feel free to express their thoughts and yet—when all is done—agree to love and work alongside the majority. When either side yields to wise counsel or, at the end of the debate, the parties come to a compromise, God cheers! Unfortunately, situations do not always resolve this easily. Trouble will occur, often the result of impure motivations, the parishioners' need for control, or unwillingness to yield to another's vision. And sometimes, heaven help us, it will come because we just plain messed up. We made the wrong decision, said the hurtful thing, or pushed forward with an ill-conceived plan out of pride. Just because your husband is God's man doesn't mean he is immune to intentional sin or pure blunder. Just because you are his wife doesn't mean you won't be tempted to react in the flesh when your hubby is called out. In her book *Counsel for Pastors' Wives*, Diane Langberg aptly states,

"Whether or not problems get out of hand is in large measure dictated by the attitudes and expectations with which one approaches ministry."[1]

Plan on Having a Plan

If you haven't figured it out yet, I am a strong believer in setting our attitudes positively where ministry is concerned. One thing that aggravates me is the abundance of material for dealing with the problems of ministry rather than proactive approaches to preventing them. The word *proactive* is one of my favorites in all the English language. It means "acting in advance to deal with an unexpected difficulty."[2] One of the main reasons I felt compelled to write this book is so you can say, "I was ready for this, and I have a plan!"

For that purpose, we are going to walk through some steps together that will help guide you through the crisis you are currently experiencing or the one that will surely come. These have become my personal ways of recognizing hot spots and how to, in one of my favorite southern sayings, go about "nippin' them in the bud."

Always use the Matthew 5 approach.

Matthew 5:23–24 instructs us, "Therefore, if you are offering your gift at the altar and there remember that your brother has something against you, leave your gift there in front of the altar. First go and be reconciled to your brother; then come and offer your gift."

I use this verse as a proactive strategy because (1) Christ commands it, and (2) defensive *re*actions are a recipe for disaster. The whole concept behind this Scripture is to be discerning when something may be amiss in a relationship with someone in the congregation and to be straightforward in dealing with it. Take care to note this Scripture doesn't say *you* should go to a sister if you are angry with *her* (though you should), but rather if you see *she* has something against *you*. In my experience, it is a very rare thing for someone to approach another and say, "There is something that is bothering me, and I'd like to talk." Our lives would be cake were it always that easy! Instead, what you will typically experience are cold shoulders, missed services, and dropped ministries. For whatever reason, mad members feel the best way to punish the preacher is to stop showing up and to simply wallow in the perceived transgression. I call these the "Silent Stewers," and to deal with them, your spiritual example will require you to suck it up and in humility make the first move even if you do not believe you've done anything wrong.

Sometimes we believe our husbands are the ones people tend to be upset with, but I have news for you. For reasons that are vastly different from those your man will face, you can inadvertently step on the toes of your church women and offend them as easily as their male counterparts. I've been criticized for anything from forgetting to pass a prayer-chain request to neglectfully allowing my kids to run through the church. However, some hurts aren't to be taken lightly. The number one reason laypeople tell me they harbor bitterness toward their pastor's wife is because she broke confidence by sharing private matters with unintended ears. Yes, girls. Our big mouths can get us in some major trouble. Can we just establish now that we should keep them shut?

For now, I certainly can't go into a laundry list of the myriad of ways you may incur another's wrath. The important thing to know is how to deal with the anger, whether you deserve it or not.

In my chatter with ministry wives, I've so often heard and thought myself, "I'm *so* tired of trying to make everyone happy. I can't be everywhere, do everything, or please every person. I didn't do anything wrong, so if someone is angry with me they can just get over it."

I understand the mind-set behind this attitude, but by expecting everyone to "get over it" and ignoring a cold shoulder, you may be brushing aside someone to whom you truly owe an apology. What am I trying to say? You don't have the option *not* to deal with it. Let me give an example of why.

There was a situation once when I noticed a friend in our congregation had pulled back from me. Like many of you, I am so incredibly busy that I tend to shy away from inviting any more drama into my life than necessary. I didn't think I had done anything to her, and frankly it was easier to pretend her distance was all in my mind. The iciness continued for a couple of months until it was obvious that whatever was going on wasn't simply a figment of my imagination. I went to my friend and told her I might be overreacting, but it seemed like she was avoiding me. I then asked if I had done or said something to offend her. She said that indeed I had and explained why. It turned out that she completely misunderstood something I'd said, but had I been in her shoes, I would have been upset too! When I asked why she hadn't come to me, she told me she figured I would think she was being petty and it wasn't worth causing a scene over. Well, it was very worth it to me to clear the air! I gave my sincerest apologies, explained what I had meant, and everything was fine again. I only wished I had said something sooner.

This minor incident is a great demonstration of the hesitancy some have in approaching you when they are troubled. You may consider your demeanor nonthreatening and welcoming, but the fact is that most people will not come to either you or your husband with their bruised feelings for the simple reason they are uncomfortable with confronting the preacher or preacher's wife. This is why you must be willing to ask God for discernment and exercise servant leadership by initiating the reconciliation.

Always take time to examine others' motives.

"What is the source of quarrels and conflicts among you? Is not the source your pleasures that wage war in your members? You lust and do not have; so you commit murder. You are envious and cannot obtain; so you fight and quarrel. You do not have because you do not ask" (James 4:1–2 NASB).

The wisdom in this Scripture says it all. Most church conflict can be boiled down to one simple word: *control*.

I once heard a story about a church considering a building program. There was one particular deacon who fiercely fought the expansion. He ranted in business meetings and generally let everyone know he didn't believe building was the right decision for the church. His view was eventually voted down, and none of the majority expected his participation with the project.

Imagine their surprise when the work began, and there stood the deacon with his tool belt on! "What are you doing here?" they asked.

His reply? "Just because I didn't agree doesn't mean I won't help. The body said 'yes,' so here I am."

And most of you are rolling your eyes right now, thinking, "Yeah, and what planet were they on because I am *so* moving there."

The Silent Stewers I mentioned earlier are actually a blessing. Most of the time you can deal with them by using the Matthew 5 strategy of talking over the problem one-on-one. However, those I refer to as "Stink Stirrers" are a different matter entirely. Their campaign for support of their own position will threaten to undermine your ministry and wreak all-out havoc in the body. Unfortunately, the Matthew 5 approach generally will not cover this one. Let me tell you why.

Instead of being like the wise deacon who accepted defeat and joined the majority, you will find Stink Stirrers take defeat personally and more often than not will invite others into their offense. Whether the decision is as simple as choosing the color of carpeting to the more complex matters of budget and programs, the sad fact is that when these people do not get their way, they will not let it go. It would be great if a temporary pout were the only result, but most of the time the fallout has longer-lasting and more far-reaching effects. I've often asked myself why church life has to be this way. My friend Tammy Nolan (wife of TNT Ministries' Tony Nolan) said it best when she told me, "Hurt people hurt people." I agree with her wholeheartedly because in my own experience, people who attack the most viciously are ones who have personal issues that go way beyond church politics.

With that said, there is an important concept every ministry wife must understand: Most assaults on your ministry aren't personal. When church members become disgruntled and lash out, it generally isn't because they don't like you—it's because they've been forced to give up an area of control. The Pharisees and Sadducees could have cared less about Jesus' teaching had it not directly threatened their influence over the people. Just as in those days, when powerful people begin losing their grip, they will automatically start looking for someone to crucify. Your hubby just happens to be the one most likely to end up as the target.

This may not encourage you one little bit, but let me tell you why it should. When we learn to separate people from their actions, it becomes much easier to love them in spite of how they hurt us. Now I'm not saying it ever gets easy to watch someone attack Luke or second-guess him when I know how he agonizes over decisions where the body is concerned. However, it helps immensely to recognize that Satan is the ultimate Stink Stirrer and accuser of the brethren. Remembering this, I can aim my righteous indignation toward him instead of allowing my unrighteous anger to be directed toward a brother or sister in Christ. If their criticisms are unfounded, then ultimately we can rely on God's justice in the matter.

However, there is an alternative consideration. What if your accusers have cause? What if you've just flat out blown it? It is a rare thing for me to hear a story of strife in the body and for a ministry wife to tell me, "We messed up." Most often we take on the countenance of a martyr and insist everyone is to blame except us, which leads to the next step in considering conflict.

Scrutinize your own motivations before you criticize others'.

In John MacArthur's *The Book on Leadership,* he sums up in a simple paragraph the major mistake of young ministers. I personally think this concept applies to ministry couples of any age, but see what you think:

> *I often tell young pastors that the fastest way to lose people's trust is not by preaching a bad sermon. People will forgive that. The fastest way to lose credibility as a leader is to make a foolish decision that leads people down a blind alley or off the end of a pier. Too many young men in ministry make impetuous and ill-considered decisions. They lead without looking where they are going. They don't count the cost. They aren't cautious enough. You might think that young leaders would make the mistake of being too timid, but in my experience, it is much more common for young men to fail because they are impetuous. They aren't sensitive. They don't seek wise counsel.*[3]

It is safe to say our nature is to assume our leadership position makes us the correct one and that anyone who disagrees hasn't prayed enough, isn't plugged in enough, or is a pawn of Satan to undermine our vision. The wise woman will stop and ask herself, "How is this situation being perceived from the other angle?" There is no shame in asking for wise counsel and accepting that you are not correct 100 percent of the time. I know that when Luke is embroiled in a complex situation he will often ask me, "Do you see something here that I don't?" It is our responsibility as ministry wives to be prayed up and honest with our husbands if God has shown you a potential misstep. It is also a huge thing for you to find a godly mentor in whom you can confide and to be willing to submit to hard truth.

In the experience I described in the opening of this chapter, I can honestly tell you that while Luke and I were in the midst of it, we couldn't see one single thing we'd done wrong. The senior pastor and his wife were the bad guys, and we were just the poor, pitiful ones who had been beaten and bruised for no apparent reason. The people who loved us naturally flocked to protect our family and, in a sense, we fed one another's offense. In this case, sadly but truly, we became the Stink Stirrers.

Now we know that although we were excusably naive, we were inexcusably wrong.

I can reflect on that time now and wish a million things. I wish the pastor had recognized that we were innocent and didn't understand church politics. I wish the church had understood that they were obligated to their pastor's opinion in calling staff. I wish we'd had one honest, unbiased person who could have told us exactly what was happening and how to avoid being crushed in the avalanche.

But none of that happened. I will tell you what did happen, though. We learned to always question ourselves first and others later. It also taught us the warning signals to recognize if this ever happens again so we can run like crazy in the other direction. We also discovered that no trial is wasted. We now look at conflict in a twofold manner by asking ourselves, "What does this mean for today, and how will it profit tomorrow?" And of one thing I am sure: God will not allow even an ounce of pain if He doesn't intend for it to produce pounds and pounds of cure.

We also exult in our tribulations, knowing
that tribulation brings about perseverance; and
perseverance, proven character; and proven character,
hope. (Rom. 5:3–4 NASB)

Support your husband? Yes! Protect him? NO!

Years ago I had a conversation with a ministry wife who proudly shared she had told off a deacon because of the way he was constantly disagreeing with her husband. At the time, Luke and I weren't on staff so I didn't consider the implications of what she said. I just knew then, as I really know now, that Luke McKay would kill me in a million different ways (okay, maybe only half a million) if I told off any man on his behalf. Or any woman, either, for that matter.

None of us has an easy time holding our tongues where our husbands and children are concerned, but hear me well when I say, "Keep that lip *zipped!*" There is one truth in Revelation we all need to keep our minds wrapped around in order to prevent an embarrassing display that will mark you as a loud-mouthed rebel and your husband as a wimp who needs his little missus to come to the rescue.

Revelation 1:20 is the last verse in John's description of the risen Lord. It reads, "As for the mystery of the seven stars which you saw *in My right hand,* and the seven golden lampstands: the seven stars are the angels of the seven churches, and the seven lampstands are the seven churches" (NASB).

I've read many commentaries on this particular passage, and most agree the angels of the churches refer to the overseers or, presently, the pastors and elders of the church.

Here's my personal interpretation (please forgive me, theologians, if this is a stretch): If Jesus Christ Himself is holding my dear husband in His righteous right hand, then I can trust Him to guide and protect him in the midst of any adversity. There have been times when people have cut Luke to the quick, and the only thing that prevented me from pinning them to the wall was the fact that Jesus already had it covered. And because we are told in Scripture that marriage is two people becoming one flesh, I believe that providential care also extends to you, dear sister, when your heart is broken and bruised. Resting in His hands and trusting Him to execute perfect justice on behalf of the innocent are what will keep our hearts and minds from responding with depression, despondency, and bitterness. If we suffer, it is imperative that we do so according to 1 Peter 3:16–17, which says to keep "a clear conscience, so that those who speak maliciously against your *good behavior* in Christ may be ashamed of their slander. It is better, if it is God's will, to suffer for doing good than for doing evil."

Our God will never let injustice reign. It may take some time, but I can tell you one thing because I've seen it happen personally: If we maintain our personal integrity and don't allow the flesh to control our actions, God Himself will convict hearts, and they will change for the better. You may never be made aware of this in your lifetime, but in the words of Dorothy Patterson, "We must forgive when no forgiveness is requested."[4] Our calling is to make sure the conviction doesn't fall on us. And it won't if we beg the Holy Spirit to aid us in keeping a clear conscience.

The girls at my blog had *so* much to say about this topic. Let's consider their insight before we move on to happier thoughts.

Round Table

- "Our former pastorate was a very troubled church, and most of the conflicts experienced there were definitely based on control issues. What amazes me is that people somehow think the church belongs to them and it is their responsibility instead of God's to control every aspect of it."—Deborah @ Chocolate and Coffee

- "Tradition had much to do with the conflict we experienced at our new church. I wish that I could say we immediately walked in love and forgiveness and prayed for our 'enemies.' At first we were very hurt and so we withdrew; then we got angry and depressed. It took much time and prayer to get to the point of healing and restoration and forgiveness."—Merrie @ Merrie Days

- "My husband was often brought into new church situations to clean up someone else's mess. We were often appointed to a church that had been suffering because of conflict. I'm convinced some parishioners thrive on conflict and won't be happy unless they are dredging up something."—Susan @ Learning for Lifetime

- "The last conflict we experienced related to a control issue with a man in our church. My husband had absolutely no support

from the deacons when it arose. It is terribly hard to serve in
a church when no one has your back."—Crystal @ Life Is
Nothing Without Him

- "I was guilty of occasionally pressuring my husband to tell me
  what was going on, more for my own 'gossip heart' than his
  well-being. I learned that I need to listen to him and not dig
  at the issues unless he asks me to."—Laura

- "One of the most important spiritual disciplines we can exercise is to release our frustrations to Jesus first. There is such
  sweet release in knowing we've invited Him into our heartaches. I also cannot stress enough the importance of finding
  a mentor or understanding person with whom you are safe to
  vent. That is one reason I am so excited about the community available through blogs. I felt somewhat isolated before,
  but now I have a great number of wise women with whom
  I can share concerns without fear of breaking confidence. It
  is also wonderful to be able to say, 'I'm going through this
  situation and I reacted like so. Was I right?' Be willing to hear
  hard truth when your own attitude is the one that needs to
  change."—Lisa

- "I couldn't agree with you more about keeping our mouths
  quiet when it comes to defending our husbands. My husband
  does not need me all in a hissy fit when we get home because
  I was in the midst of trying to hold up the shield and everything else. He needs a place of refuge, my loving and wise

support, a new and fresh place to share his heart without the criticism he just faced being acted out by his wife."—Kelli @ Ponderings of a Pastor's Wife

- "We had a lot of conflict in our first church. At the time I thought it was all the church's fault. Looking back—and with the hard but true words from my mentor (also a pastor's wife)—I see where I was just as much the problem if not more than the people at the church. My husband is a student minister, and one woman constantly attacked him. I knew he was doing the best he could, and I was so mad that she did not think it was good enough. There were Sundays that I did not go to church because I knew if I did see her, words would fly out of my mouth that should never be there in the first place! I wish I could say that I had complete control over my tongue now, but that is not the case! I am much further along than before but I still have to rein it in a lot. Now when I am frustrated I vent to my husband and my mentor."—Lori @ Welcome to My World

Now That You Know:

1. Describe a season of church conflict you've experienced either as a minister or member. What did you learn from the experience? If the conflict still colors how you operate within the church, confess that to Jesus. Be honest with your feelings, but don't allow Satan to feed your offense. Seek out a wise pastor's wife who will help you work through these hard days.

2. Children do not have the ability to separate people from their actions. If someone is making their dad stressed or their mom cry, they know nothing but to be angry. Many preachers' kids say the way their parents were treated in the church drove them from it as adults. Guard young children's ears and hearts as much as possible. Make an effort to remain positive in front of teens.

3. Guard your tongue! I can't stress enough the damage that can be done when we speak first and think later. If in doubt, don't say it. If your heart is pounding in anger, turn and walk away. Tell it to Jesus. He alone can calm your heart.

4. Laypeople: I don't know if you can fully comprehend the good intentions your ministry family has toward you. No pastor ever came to a church with the motivation of

tearing it to pieces. Give him and his family the benefit of the doubt. If you perceive a misstep, approach it gently, giving room for correction. Be open to something new. You may be amazed at what God will do when you allow Him to be the only One in control.

Five

I Can Have BFFs in the Church Pews

True friendship is the least jealous of loves. Two friends
delight to be joined by a third, and three by a fourth.
—C. S. Lewis, The Four Loves

My husband would agree that I have a laundry list of eccentricities, but perhaps one of the strangest is a phobia of people breathing directly into my face. At the risk of my confession convincing you I'm a total weirdo, the reason is I'm afraid if I inhale too much of another person's exhaled carbon dioxide, I'll smother. In my estimation, you may as well lock me in a garage with the car running. Carbon dioxide, carbon monoxide. It's all the same to me.

I told you I was weird. Will you keep reading anyway?

This little quirk is particularly problematic for a woman who spends the bulk of her days sharing limited parsonage space with five other humans—all of whom feel it necessary to breathe her air while they are talking to her. It's not that I don't want them near; it just really freaks me out to be in their cloud of exhaust.

I've come up with a dorky little game to play with the kids to mask my neurosis. When they have spent too much time in my air supply, I flail my arms like a mad woman and yell, "If I can hit you, you're too close!" The kids think it is hilarious and try their hardest to see just how near me they can get without getting whacked. The hubby isn't quite as amused.

And such is the way we often operate in churches where friendships are concerned. Both ministry wives and laypeople are actually trained to fear intimacy. Because of this, we flap our arms shouting, "I'm not sure if I can trust you, so keep clear!" At the same time, the church members swat back, assuring us, "No worries! I don't *want* to get close because you'll just leave me eventually anyway!" And so we carry on like a room full of crazed dodo birds staying far enough away from one another to avoid getting hurt.

Sad, isn't it?

It would be if this were the way we *had* to operate—but it isn't. I'm convinced if we exercise biblical wisdom and use good common sense, we can find plenty of BFFs (a rather juvenile abbreviation for best friends forever) in our own church pews.

Jesus Needed Friends Too

If there is one Person who can sympathize with the need for friends in the midst of ministry, it is our Lord Jesus. In *The Training of the Twelve,* A. B. Bruce points out the necessity of close comrades:

It is probable that the selection of a limited number
to be His close and constant companions had become
a necessity to Christ, in consequence of His very
success in gaining disciples. His followers, we imagine,
had grown so numerous as to be an encumbrance
and an impediment to His movements, especially
in the long journeys which mark the later part of
His ministry. … But it was His wish that certain
selected men should be with Him at all times and
in all places,—His traveling companions in all His
wanderings, witnessing all His work, and ministering
to His daily needs.[1]

Now obviously I am not suggesting ministers are entitled to an entourage. Jesus stated He did not come into the world to be served but to serve—the same motivation anyone who presumes to labor in His name should have. As the crowd grew and demanded more and more of Jesus' time, it became apparent that in His humanness He needed help. However, I'm convinced He wasn't just looking for a logistics team; He was looking for comrades as well. The intensity of Jesus' daily schedule demanded that He decompress—first through time spent with His Father and then with a band of men who could share a belly laugh or a great meal. I believe even the Savior of the universe needed a safe place where He could kick back and simply be a carpenter from Nazareth.

Ministry families need these same types of relationships, and yet finding and maintaining them can be tricky. Spend too much time with one family and you are being exclusive. Don't spend enough time with a family and you are an elitist. And then there are those times when we've risked letting down our guards only to be burned crispier than a forgotten hot dog on a campfire.

And frankly, that stinks. (Hardy, har.)

So how do we go about finding BFFs in the church? What should you look for in a friend? What type of friend should *you* be? How do you avoid being exclusive or reclusive to the detriment of your church? Let's use examples from one of the most famous friendships in Scripture—that of David and Jonathan—as a guide.

Uncommon Friends, Common Faith

Even though David had been serving intermittently in Saul's court, he and Jonathan first met after David's stunning victory over Goliath. First Samuel 18:1 tells us, "Now it came about when [David] had finished speaking to Saul, that the soul of Jonathan was knit to the soul of David, and Jonathan loved him as himself" (NASB).

Have you ever met someone and instantly clicked? Been introduced to a sister in Christ and within five minutes were chatting like old friends? C. S. Lewis rightly said, "Friendship is born at that moment when one person says to another, 'What! You too? I thought I was the only one.'" There is an instant bonding when we know we are not alone in our passions and pains. Jonathan listened to David and Saul speaking and obviously could tell from the grace in David's speech that he and this man had much in common—so much so that from this point forward his well-being was directly bound in David's.

There were many reasons Jonathan could have resisted friendship with David—not the least of which was the fact that David was a threat to Jonathan's present influence and future kingship. Likewise, David knew he'd been anointed as Saul's replacement, so becoming bosom buddies with the man who, in the normal course of things, should become the next king seems a conflict of interests. However, the two of them recognized qualities in one another that transcended earthly difficulties. Sometimes the hard thing is just flat out worth it.

And so are friendships between servant leaders and laypeople.

Sadly, our seminaries and even other pastors' wives may counsel against becoming close to women in our churches. When I was young in ministry, I had one person tell me there should always be a wall between me and the other women in the congregation and that I should learn to expect and embrace loneliness. I appreciate her point of view but—call me a rebel—I will never wrap myself in a life of isolation. Though there will be times when you and your husband will be forced to deal with an ordeal alone due to the sensitivity of a situation, this is not commonplace. I can't imagine God ever intended for us to live life according to an exception rather than the rule. We are called to walk in faith in all areas of life, and our relationships are perhaps one of the chief places trust in God's involvement is needed.

How David and Jonathan Succeeded

There were many ways the friendship between David and Jonathan met their personal needs in addition to fulfilling God's plans for their lives and for the nation of Israel. Here are but a few characteristics of their relationship that caused it to work in spite of the odds stacked against them:

Their friendship was founded on a common devotion to God.

Jonathan recognized David's great love for God while witnessing the conversation between Saul and David after he defeated Goliath. No doubt David recounted the battle to Saul, not hesitating to give God the glory for the display of His might through a young shepherd. David was willing to risk life and limb in order to defend the name of the Lord. David's loyalty to God in spite of his personal safety had to be one of the things that drew Jonathan to him.

I can't even begin to tell you how many women I've met within the churches we've served whose testimonies have affected me greatly. I am naturally drawn to these kinds of people because they inspire and challenge my own walk with the Lord and make me want to step it up. These can be women of any age, but I deeply respect the senior women as great pillars of faith. They aren't afraid to proclaim the goodness of God toward them, nor are they too busy to share it. I've made a point in my relationships within the church to make sure I never isolate myself from women who are my seniors and also to be forever willing to accept their wise counsel. We younger ministry wives (and our husbands!) can sometimes feel intimidated by the older segment of our congregations for fear they don't respect us because of our age or seeming inexperience—much like young Timothy in Scripture (1 Tim. 4:12). There is no shame in submitting to our wiser sisters as mothers in the Lord in a Titus 2 relationship, remembering that by honoring these women we are displaying an awesome example of servant leadership.

You may be in a situation where there are very few women your age to befriend. If that is the case, please don't neglect the gift God has given you in the senior women who are most eager to pet and love your family to death. If you are the senior woman, know there are women in your church who crave your insight and advice whether they know how to ask for it or not.

Age is but one factor that can possibly hinder friendships. God may send you to a place where cultural differences (especially for our missionary sisters), regional customs (as in the northern and southern U.S.), or even societal views (congregations more steeped in idealism regarding separation from the culture, etc.) may give you the feeling you have nothing in common with the women there. As long as you have faith, you have something to talk about. Let that be your jumping-off place, and then ask God to open doors of friendship and mentorship.

Their confidence in one another was based on personal history.

In 1 Samuel 20, David fled to Jonathan to find out why Saul was trying to kill him—again. At first Jonathan defended his father by saying, "My father does nothing either great or small without disclosing it to me. So why should my father hide this thing from me? It is not so!" (1 Sam. 20:2 NASB).

At this point, David vowed to Jonathan his accusation was true. David's declaration went way beyond the "I'm tellin' you, your daddy is trying to stab me!" we might use in a similar situation today. To put oneself under oath was to invite God's involvement and appeal to Him as the enforcement power and the all-knowing judge of human actions.[2]

That oath had to stop Jonathan in his tracks. He knew of David's unwavering trust in God and of David's own unquestionable integrity. Based on all Jonathan had observed in David's character, David's willingness to call on God as witness confirmed his accusation was true. Jonathan believed David even if that meant siding against his own father. Bless Jonathan for *wanting* to believe Saul, but Saul's past actions hardly gave Jonathan much to work with.

This matter of trust is foundational in any friendship, but it is particularly important where servant leaders and laypeople are concerned. I have often been wrongly hesitant to really open myself to women in our congregations for fear they would discover I was a mere mortal with hurts and hang-ups (and bizarre phobias). It's almost like discovering your doctor failed Anatomy 101. Can you have confidence in his diagnosis when he doesn't have the credentials to back it up? That type of fear is what caused me to hold back rather than to admit I was imperfect and risk how that would affect our ministry. Could church members follow a man whose wife sometimes missed her quiet times and had leftover chicken nuggets from the last fast-food kid's meal under the seats of her car? I didn't know because I didn't give myself the chance to find out.

And on the flip side, though I can't say I've ever had it happen to me personally, there are those women who will try to befriend the wives of the ministers because of a seeming "inside track" they may gain. I've heard tales ranging from women who want their husbands to be nominated for church office to others, looking for some perceived privilege, going out of their way in order to make strategic girlfriends out of the wives of leadership. Either of these scenarios absolutely cracks me up. Obviously these women do not realize that most of us can hardly persuade our husbands to take out the garbage, much less influence church politics. Maybe you megachurch wives have women around you who feel the need to brag about being your friend. But something tells me you are able to see through that pretty quickly and spend time with people who are more interested in your heart than your name.

The truth of the matter is that you will never know who you can trust until you open yourself up to find out. Will you get burned? At some point, yes. David never knew from one moment to the next if Saul was his friend or if he would try to stick him to the wall with his spear. But just like David and Jonathan, you have to be willing to risk in order to build some mileage into your relationships. Once you've done that, when hard days come you will have the necessary history to know whom you can rely upon. I love how one of my blog friends, Christie, stated it. She said, "I have found out that the only women I will trust with anything personal are the ones that pray with me. Not just the surface prayers, but the ones that are actually on their knees with me. It is hard to betray someone with whom you have talked with God." Amen, sister.

Their commitment to one another and God was constantly renewed.

When I was in grade school, best-friend bracelets were all the rage. You were a nobody if you didn't have one of those colored rings around your wrist. If you were truly loved, then you had a collection. However, a bracelet wasn't a sure sign of loyalty because the same fickle girl who placed that band on your arm could also jerk it away at a moment's notice for the smallest crime. Did you play with someone else at recess? Dare to talk to a sworn enemy? Well, you'd better be prepared to be bare-armed—a fate worse than death for a young girl who just wanted to belong.

Jonathan also gave David a symbol of his commitment to their friendship, but it was hardly something as unpredictable as a BFF bracelet. We are told in 1 Samuel 18:4 that Jonathan "stripped himself of the robe that was on him and gave it to David, with his armor, including his sword and his bow and his belt" (NASB).

This gift was to ratify the covenant Jonathan and David made with one another and most likely was also a sign that Jonathan understood and accepted the fact that David would follow Saul as king. We should all strive to be leaders unafraid to humbly submit to our Christian sisters with this kind of love and loyalty.

Balancing Your "Five"

Motivational speaker Jim Rohn says, "You are the average of the five people you spend the most time with." I find that concept very interesting, and in several ways, I agree. I think it is important in any friendship, not just ones within your church, to constantly evaluate its purpose. I find that I need a balance of different types of friends. I need people in my life who challenge me to run harder after God. I love having girlfriends who make me laugh my head off. I also enjoy being in mentoring relationships. There are people we need and those who need us. I find if I spend a great deal of time around people I need, I become needy and begin feeling that I have nothing to offer. Likewise, if I am constantly pouring into people who crave something from me with no comic relief, I get drained, and ministry becomes a chore instead of a delight.

Why am I telling you this? Because if you are doing the friend thing correctly within your church, you will find your circle is constantly evolving as you evaluate with whom you are spending the bulk of your time. I'm in no way trying to tell you that you can't or won't have women in your life who are constants. Handled wisely, you can have constants without having a clique. David and Jonathan had periods of time when they were together and also circumstances that demanded they separate. The wonderful thing is each time they reunited, the covenant bond between them was renewed based on a mutual, mature understanding that their current purpose didn't always include daily contact. I have so many great friends I don't get to talk with as much as I'd like, but when we do get together it's like we never parted. Those types of mature friendships will be uncommon, but they will be rarer still if we never risk enough to find them.

The Dilemma We All Face

It's very easy for me to tell you how you should just get out there and find yourself a friend. In a perfect world, you could do just that, and this problem of isolation that many ministry wives face would be a thing of the past. Because I've been there, I understand there are sensitive situations that make that all but impossible. Our precious missionary wives, especially those serving under the radar, are prime examples of women who are not able to run out and have a Starbucks with a Christian sister. And then there is the predicament so many of us face—that of needing to spill our hearts without fear of consequences to someone who understands our unique position. Even if you have other friends who are also serving in ministry, oftentimes their churches are close to yours, so talking about a temporary aggravation you may be feeling with some form of church politics can actually damage the reputation of your congregation. So what's a girl to do?

Virtual BFFs

About fifteen years ago, a guy friend of mine met a girl through an online computer dating service and brought her home to meet his parents. They married soon after.

Back then I thought that was the freakiest thing I'd ever heard. A mail-order bride? What if she were really an ax murderer? In the Witness Protection Program? Running from the long arm of the law? Couldn't he find a perfectly normal wife close to home?

She turned out to be wonderful, and the couple is still married today.

Since that time, online communities of all types have grown exponentially, and having "computer friends" is not quite as weird as it used to be. (Just don't ask my husband's opinion. He calls my blog girls "imaginary friends.") The technological age has shrunk our world so that I can now have acquaintances from New Zealand to South Africa and chat with them over my morning Diet Coke in much the same way I would with a next-door neighbor.

While I am in no way suggesting we should replace flesh-and-blood relationships with virtual ones, I can tell you they are a wonderful complement. What's even cooler is when you have the opportunity to meet face-to-face. I just returned from a trip to San

Antonio, Texas, where I met dozens of girls I've been conversing with online for over a year now. Now that we've hugged and laughed together, I consider them my real-life friends.

Of these girls, most know nothing about my church, and I feel free to share details of difficult situations, knowing they will pray and give wise counsel on how to cope. The freedom they've given me to vent is just one of the reasons I created a blogroll of ministry wives as a resource for finding one another and forming these types of bonds. I can't tell you the number of emails I've received from wives whose husbands have been ensnared in sin or whose ministries are going through intense struggle, and who feel they have no one they can tell these awful details to without being judged. We all need a safe place and, if you don't have that in the girl next door, perhaps you can find one in a girl half a country away. It works for me. Maybe it can for you, too.

Of course, there are many other ways to connect with other women walking in your shoes. In Lorna Dobson's book *I'm More Than the Pastor's Wife,* she encourages ministry wives to pray about beginning a support group to encourage, edify, and comfort one another. These groups can take on many forms—book clubs, monthly luncheons, just-for-fun activities, etc. The key is to remain flexible and open to the needs of the women who agree to meet. You can find more information about this book in the Resources section.

Keep Your Head Out of the Sand

There are so many areas of church life where we can feel nitpicked to death. When it comes down to the lay perspective on something as personal as our friendships, it is so easy to want to shut down and ignore whether our actions are causing hurt feelings—justified or not. In wrapping up our discussion on friends in the church, allow me to give a few pointers on practically managing the buddy system:

You are always an example whether you want to be or not.

In other words—remember yourself! We have friends who sometimes get out of hand. They watch things we don't. Say things we wouldn't—or shouldn't. But that doesn't mean we don't love them or still spend time with them. It can be easy to get drawn into laughing at coarse talk or even gossip if you aren't mindful of the example you are setting. Never let your temporary approval of bad behavior be someone else's justification for continuing in it.

On the other hand, don't be offended when your friends seem to guard their conversation just because you are the preacher's wife. I have a standard response when someone says, "Oops, I'd better not say that; Lisa is standing here." I typically say something along the lines of, "Well, if Jesus doesn't mind you saying it then why in the world should I care?"

That gets 'em every time.

Don't isolate yourself with one person or group of people.

The number one complaint I hear from laypeople where ministry-wife friendships are concerned is the feeling she is part of a clique. Obviously there are going to be women with whom you have more in common, but it is your responsibility as a servant leader to leave yourself open to new relationships with a diverse group of people.

If you are accused of having a clique, many times it is from someone who feels she isn't in it. However, if you'll follow Rohn's "Five Friends" concept we talked about earlier in this chapter, I sincerely doubt you'll have this problem. I asked a straightforward, tell-it-like-it-is woman in our church if she perceived I had a clique. She replied, "Lisa, I know you have some girlfriends you spend time with more than others. But I see you accepting invitations to the senior ladies' events. I see you teaching groups from children through grown women. I see you welcoming visitors and having lunch with them. So I would say absolutely not. But don't you ever let what people think of you keep you from doing what you want with whom you want." I was nervous when I asked the question because I didn't want to find I was a big hypocrite. Her encouragement means the world to me and, by the way, she is definitely one of my BFFs!

Accept invitations!

I know this advice may fly right in the face of everything else I have told you or will soon tell you about learning when to say no and not feeling obligated to attend every function. However, there is no other way you will ever get to know the women of your church unless you spend a little time with them outside of the normal worship times. Within reason, go to the Sunday school parties. Attend the bridal luncheons. Celebrate the new babies. You will endear yourself and your husband to the congregation by making an effort to know them on their turf. I'm a strategic attendee. If my schedule is overwhelmed and

I can hit one event that may allow me to visit with more than one member of the same clan—a child's birthday party, for instance—then I will choose that over trying to plan something one-on-one.

Avoid withdrawing when wounded.

There will no doubt arrive a point in church life when you will be hurt. Treachery will come. Impure motivations will be revealed. The girl you thought you could trust with your heart will rip it out and stomp on it. Psalm 55:12–14 says,

> *If an enemy were insulting me,*
> *I could endure it;*
> *if a foe were raising himself against me,*
> *I could hide from him.*
> *But it is you, a man like myself,*
> *my companion, my close friend,*
> *with whom I once enjoyed sweet fellowship*
> *as we walked with the throng at the house of God.*

Most of us can relate to the heart-wrenching pain the psalmist experienced when betrayed by someone with whom he had worshipped.

Our first instinct during these times is to pull back into our shell and say, "Never again!" I've heard it over and over from my ministry girlfriends. Someone in the church broke their hearts, and the answer to preventing it from happening again is to withdraw. They may not be in danger of being hurt again, but what does it gain? Pain free does not equal happy no matter how you try to add it up.

What if the apostle Paul had quit when those who had worked closely with him in ministry maligned him? What a loss if he had cut himself off forever from Mark instead of allowing a reconciliation that resulted in a deep appreciation and friendship. What if he'd said, "No more!" after he'd gotten one beating too many? He could have settled into a nice home in the Judean countryside with nary a stoning or whipping in sight. However, he knew his calling wasn't in safety but in sacrifice. You will never be content on the sidelines when God has called you to the field.

The Ultimate Friend

No chapter on friendship could be complete without a reminder of our need for intimacy with Christ. He is indeed a friend who will stick closer than a brother—or sister. There are times when no one will have the capacity to meet your need except for Him. I promise you that when your needs are being met by Christ, you'll learn to expect less from other people and be more appreciative when they offer more than anticipated.

Because I believe being a great pastor's wife is directly related to the intimacy of our friendship with Christ, I've listed some of my favorite reading in the Resources section of this book. Stay on your knees and in the Word. You'll always find a friend waiting there.

Round Table

The M2M Girls, both ministry and laypeople, commented more on this topic than any other. Sound off, girlfriends!

- "I know we were told in seminary not to make close friends in the congregation, but rules were made to be broken! Actually, I think times have changed. We have always had close friends in our congregation. We don't hang out with them all the time at church events; in fact, we hardly see each other there. But we do spend time together 'after hours,' so to speak."—Robin @ Robinznest

- "I have had close friends in every church where my husband has pastored, but I have been burned as well. The cardinal rule is never, ever, ever talk badly about another staff person or any member of their family. (Not that we would ever do that, right?) The staff should always present a united front."—Jeannette @ Abound in Hope

- "Popularity cliques that can occur with the pastor's wife are not good. In my in-laws' church, the pastor's wife is downright rude to anyone not in her clique. It's embarrassing to watch and would definitely prevent me from ever being interested in joining that church."—Lydia (layperson)

- "I have, in all honesty, given up on having BFFs in the church we pastor. I have been burned and feel it is best to develop those friendships with other ministers' wives or ladies outside the church."—Cassandra @ Tripping Around the Sun

- "I do have a dear friend at our church. She's someone I can confide in. I would go crazy without her. I don't know if it's worth mentioning, but I'm thirty and she's, well, about twice my age."—R-Liz @ Catharsis & Son

- "I have seen women try and cozy up to me, then I find out they are really trying to get me to manipulate my husband to do something that would be for their benefit—usually some program or ministry they want started or a complaint about someone, etc."—Kim @ Little Sanctuary

- "I believe ministry wives should have friends within the church. I can't imagine that they should have to feel the need to go outside the 'home church family' to have a couple of best friends. I would think that would make them feel disconnected from the body."—His Life for Mine (layperson, name withheld)

- "I consider myself friends of two of our pastors' wives. I often think about how difficult it must be for them with such a large congregation (4,000+). Both of these ladies have other friends who are more their BFFs, but I have never felt they played favorites. If I need urgent prayer, I call these women and they are ON IT and they will come over immediately if I need them."—Michelle V @ Michelle V's Blog

- "I'm mad because you didn't speak to me at church this Sunday. Ha Ha Ha! Just kidding!"—Brooke (one of my many wisecracking church BFFs) @ The Mail Girl

Now That You Know:

1. Do you have someone you would consider a close friend within your church? If not, what is your reason for holding back? If you are new in a congregation, don't be afraid to take the first step. Arrange a playdate or a girls' night out for the general population and see who shows up. Your new BFF might be within that group.

2. Consider blogging as a tool useful in forming meaningful friendships. Not sure if it's for you? Go to APreachersWife.com and click on the "Married to the Ministry" blogroll button for links to hundreds of ministry-wife blogs. I promise you will have much in common with the great girls listed in this directory.

3. Laypeople: In what ways have you reached out to your pastor's wife? I promise you she wants someone to reach out to her—especially if she is shy! Invite her out to lunch or a movie or shopping. She needs you as much as you need her.

Six

HOW TO EMBRACE
MY OWN THING

A need does not constitute a call.
—Author unknown

In the early days of ministry, no one told me it was acceptable to do My Own Thing.

As a relatively new Christian, I'm not sure I had any concept of personal ministry. While I agree my chief role has always been to support Luke in God's calling on his life, I went completely overboard and laid aside the woman I had been, assuming the identity of one I barely recognized. In some regards that was a very good thing, but I missed parts of that girl, and I wasn't quite sure how to get her back.

I've shared that my marriage to Luke didn't have the best of beginnings. We had been Christians for only a year when God overwhelmingly confirmed His path for us. My former "friends" assured me there was no way the preacher-wife thing would stick for long. I was determined to prove them wrong and to make Luke look good at all costs—even if that meant taking on activities I didn't necessarily like. Who wouldn't love a pastor whose wife simultaneously led the women's ministry, directed vacation Bible school, taught Sunday school, served in the nursery, and cooked for every potluck and funeral in her spare time? For Luke's sake I did what I felt I had to do—I got busy.

The Reasons for Yes

Over the years, the motivation to take on activities that are beyond my calling has changed. In the beginning, I was driven by fear with a side order of obligation. Now, the portions of that combo have been reversed. I find myself saying yes to activities that are Not My Thing because I don't want a vital ministry of the church to be dropped for lack of someone to run it. (Nonvital ministries do not merit this much energy. I'll explain the difference in a bit.) This is known as the "I'll Do It Since No One Else Will" phenomenon. Perhaps you are familiar with it?

As a very current example, our public school system has a program called Bible Release Time. Each week, students whose parents give permission come to our church (next door to the elementary school) for a Bible class in place of their PE class. Unheard of, right? Running this program requires someone willing to teach five age-graded classes back-to-back every Thursday. Up until the time of this writing, those people have been Luke and me.

We have made the request numerous times for someone to take over the program. There has been some temporary help but nothing that would release us from this duty. Because the ministry requires an entire weekday, it has been very difficult to find someone willing or able to help. Luke and I have loaded plates, but if we say no, the outreach to these precious kids will be lost. We've tried to lay it down and see what happens, but, invariably, no one steps up and we are left holding the lesson book once again.

These are the kinds of situations where there is no easy answer. No doubt you find yourself in this same predicament time after time. At what point does one lay an entire ministry at the feet of Jesus and trust someone to be obedient and take it? Worse yet, if that person doesn't step forward and we are firm with our own no, what does it say about our church if one of its primary evangelistic ministries is discontinued for lack of volunteers?

Sigh.

I share this dilemma because it would be very easy for me to write a chapter telling you to just say no, when in reality it isn't always that easy. On the other hand, we can also be guilty of assuming there is no one to take the reins while that person is in our pews just waiting for someone to ask her to exercise her gifts. And then there are those times when we can use Not My Thing to mask disobedience.

Yes, that ouches me, too.

Most ministry wives I know are in desperate need of a practical way to determine what activities and ministries they should accept. Using the Bible Release Time (BRT) scenario as a jumping-off point, I'm going to give you some tools to help with that very difficult process.

Sharing the Word—Even When It Hurts

When I originally took on the BRT ministry, Luke and I were new to the church and the youth pastor who had previously directed it had just resigned. The school year was about to begin, so it was imperative we come up with a teacher—and fast!

I loved the idea of our church having the privilege of sharing the gospel with hundreds of children each week, and overwhelmingly this was the reason I said yes. However, there were subreasons I've not been as quick to confess until now.

I didn't yet know the people in our church or their hearts toward me. Each week as the request for help was made, in my mind I could hear them thinking, "Lisa doesn't have a job. Why doesn't she just do it?" And then I would wonder how Luke would look if one of the first events under his leadership was the collapse of one of the church's signature ministries. (Not to mention it was one of the only ones that existed to serve unbelievers, as opposed to the many that catered to the comfort of the body.) It rarely occurs to a ministry family that the congregation should accept a portion of the blame if a program dissolves. It rarely occurs to the congregation, either. I have found most people are content to blame the preacher—especially the preacher himself.

To put an end to The Voices, I took over the ministry thinking that would buy some time until someone came along and relieved me of this duty. That was three years ago, and here I sit.

As I process what I did versus what I should have done, I wonder if the two options are complete opposites or if they are one and the same. Translated: Did I do the right thing by taking the responsibility, or should I have assumed that BRT had run its course within our church and it was time to let go? Was it some fluke this opportunity presented itself to me, or did God orchestrate it as a vehicle of obedience and a training ground for the future? This is a very specific example, but I would like to use it as a litmus test of sorts to help determine how to wisely apply our yes and no.

Just Say No and Be Done with It?

The reason I face such a dilemma where BRT is concerned is because of its primary purpose—sharing the gospel and making disciples. As believers of Christ, our highest calling and privilege is the Great Commission. We are commanded to live lives characterized by professing our hope, and yet far too often we allow the fear of rejection or excessive busyness to cause us to tuck our salvation safely away in the recesses of our hearts.

At the risk of revealing too much of my selfish nature, I confess to you that in my flesh I no longer want to teach BRT. It wears me out. It takes preparation time away from other studies I'd like to be writing. I can't plan a thing on Thursdays for nine solid months out of the year. *But,* if I apply the Not My Thing excuse to this captive audience of hundreds of school children each week, I lose the opportunity for a major part of my personal witness. When I pray over this situation, it occurs to me that God has given me this opportunity to have significant impact and be obedient to the Great Commission within steps outside my back door. Could it get any easier? Also, His Spirit tells me Satan will fight to claim my will where sharing Christ's name is concerned.

Many responses from my blog expressed how aggravating it is for people to hide behind the mask of calling when, in fact, they just don't want to work. This can be true for laypeople and ministry families. Often we wear ourselves out in the world so that there's no energy left for the church. This is a constant struggle for me considering I have four children—three of whom are involved in every sport the school and recreation league offers. One of my frequent prayers is for God to place a zeal for His house back in the hearts of men and women (Ps. 26:8). That we would look forward to being there instead of thinking of meeting times as an interruption to our weeks. That we would never equate *hard* with Not My Thing.

We are not called to make disciples—we are commanded! It is natural that Satan will attack those desires and fatigue us with the thoughts of pouring it out week after week. Yes, our first duty is to our families, and I'm in no way suggesting you should take on an activity to the detriment of your husband and children. But does our vision for our family align with our purpose as believers? Are we teaching our children the importance of Christian service or of playdate and ball-game attendance?

Okay, my purpose here is not to go off on a tangent but rather to use the example as a springboard for answering this vital question: Will laying aside a ministry or choosing not to participate keep people from hearing the gospel or you from being obedient in sharing it? If yes, give serious thought before making that decision. You just may find God intended for you to cut out some nonessential busyness to focus on something more divine. In my case, though I've dreaded many Thursdays, joy always comes in the morning—especially when my yes to God plays some small part in one of the kids saying yes to Him too.

The decision I've made to continue the BRT ministry has been a hard one for me to work through, but ultimately I know I am doing what God has ordained for me right now. However, you should know that in the event God transfers that burden to someone else I am *so* out of there. Hashing the thing out with Him, though, has helped me rightly judge the importance of other things that beg for my attention. He's also taught me that if I am relieved of this work, I should immediately replace it with another soul-winning one and not use the free time to haul my kids to one more sporting event or go shopping at Target.

Unless…. Do you think Jesus would care if I evangelized the shoe department? That would give new meaning to the phrase "walking the aisle," and you know I'm all for relevance.

The Unashamed "No"

Let's consider the flip side of this coin: When is it necessary and perfectly acceptable to say no? Philippians 2:12–13 says, "Therefore, my dear friends, as you have always obeyed—not only in my presence, but now much more in my absence—continue to work out your salvation with fear and trembling, for it is God who works in you to will and to act according to his good purpose." The desire to work out our salvation is a gift of God, but, as I've already suggested to you, Satan is at war in our will particularly where sharing the gospel of Christ is concerned. For that reason, we must be very cautious in passing up opportunity for proclaiming His name unless we are replacing it with another outlet to do so.

However, we cannot ignore the wisdom of Romans 12:6–8 where operating within our call is concerned. I've always loved *The Message* translation, which instructs,

*If you preach, just preach God's Message, nothing
else; if you help, just help, don't take over; if you
teach, stick to your teaching; if you give encouraging
guidance, be careful that you don't get bossy; if
you're put in charge, don't manipulate; if you're
called to give aid to people in distress, keep your eyes
open and be quick to respond; if you work with the
disadvantaged, don't let yourself get irritated with
them or depressed by them. Keep a smile on your face.*

This passage suggests a few things I think are important to note:

God's call is focused.

Women's Bible teacher Beth Moore once said you "can't do a thousand things to the glory of God."[1] Truer words have never been spoken. The most important thing a minister's wife can do from the outset is determine her spiritual gifts and practice them with excellence and simplicity. Don't know what Your Thing is? Take a Spiritual Gifts Inventory. A free, online version is available at Ephesians Four Ministries (www.ChurchGrowth.org). Once you've discovered how to mesh your God-given abilities with areas of service it will be much easier to say no when requests come that are Not Your Thing.

I must also say I am supremely blessed to have a husband who doesn't expect me to fill in gaps. He knows my proclivity to say yes when we both know I'm stretched as it is. He is very bold in communicating that the only thing he expects from me is to be his wife and the kids' mother and that everyone should take that into consideration. He is also perfectly okay with my throwing him under the bus if need be to keep me from overobligation. How? I blame my "no" on him, citing something along the lines of "Luke McKay will choke me if I take on one more thing." Which is not such a stretch.

Our call can be distorted by ambition—our own or someone else's. I've had many conversations with people who've given me great ideas about new things our church should be doing. They typically don't want to *do* what they've suggested; they just want someone to get it done—namely Luke and me. One woman presented a request to me as a way to "enhance our church's standing in the community." The motivation was to glorify our church's name—not Christ's. Once upon a time her suggestions would have sounded intriguing. There was nothing overtly evil in them. Once upon a time, I may have felt the need to try to accommodate her requests for no other reason than *she* thought I should. Thankfully, I've realized that the only way I'll have my "happily ever after" is for God to write the story.

I've learned to deal with these situations by operating under the assumption these people are describing their grand plans because God is asking them to step into something more. Luke always says, "If God gave you the idea, then He's probably telling you to do it!" I've come a long way in saying, "You know, that's a fabulous idea. I'll support and pray for you if you decide to take that on." There have been times when the person has blossomed into new ministry. And the others? Well, they are too ashamed to admit they never intended on serving. This will be a boundary issue you'll deal with time and time again, so preparing a standard comeback will help you in saying no without being downright rude.

Just like the woman who wanted to glorify our church's name, ministers can also be guilty of overworking themselves to glorify their own. In a culture filled with Christian superstars, it can be so tempting to do whatever it takes to draw numbers instead of make disciples. It is well within our bounds to help our hubby recognize if his joy—or lack of it—seems to be coming more from filled pews than changed lives. It is also our responsibility to keep check on our hearts to be certain this mentality doesn't become ours as well.

Depression can expose our call.

Depression is a complicated illness, so let me state clearly I am no authority on the subject nor am I offering any medical advice. However, since I've suffered from bouts of it, I feel I can share a bit of what I've learned from the experience.

I've been in many funks, but the most prolonged one took place when our family moved to North Carolina to attend seminary. We had three sons, ages four, two, and two months. God had confirmed that He intended for Luke to pursue a graduate degree, but that didn't negate the fact we were moving away from our hometown where we'd just resettled after four years in college. We were forced to move from a great house we'd completely remodeled to a tiny campus apartment. We went from two cars to one. Luke took the one car, attended school all day, and worked at night—leaving me home alone with the kids at least twelve to fourteen hours per day. The cost of living was exorbitant compared to the small Kentucky town where we had attended college. Luke's pay covered only half of our monthly expenses, and with three preschoolers there wasn't a job anywhere I could take that would cover daycare, much less the cost of another car to get me to work and back. And needless to say, retail therapy for my blues was not an option.

On top of all that, my oldest son did not handle the move well at all. He missed his grandparents, his cousins, and his John Deere bedroom, and he didn't have the capability to understand why life had changed so drastically overnight. His constant smile turned to endless tears, and it was just about all I could take.

My days grew darker and darker. The housework piled up. The kids and I stayed in our pajamas most of the day, and I began having severe stomach problems that resulted in acute vomiting episodes. Luke was worried out of his mind about us all and could scarcely concentrate on school because his family appeared to be falling to pieces right in front of his eyes. Both of us prayed to God in question marks. We thought we had done what He asked of us, so what in the world was the deal?

It was during those days of crying out to Him that I decided to put my feelings on paper. For the first time in my Christian life, there was no one to hash out the hard things with except God Himself. He and I wrestled, and like Jacob, I decided in the midst of the striving I wasn't letting go until He blessed me.

It was a short time later I met a girl in our apartment building who was experiencing my exact emotions. We would meet up on the playground and mope because our husbands were gone in our only vehicles while we kept the home fires burning … or not. I knew she was having a terrible time adjusting, and so one day I decided to email her a devotion of sorts that I had written mostly to myself.

Her response blew me away. She told me how God spoke to her so clearly through the email and how much she appreciated having specific verses to apply to her pain. She told me she smiled for the first time in days. To God be the glory.

I already had a small taste of women's ministry in college, but most of my work there was centered on event planning and leading studies from other writers. It never occurred to me that maybe I could prepare my own and that God would ask me to minister to women through the written word. The elation I felt over being used of God to encourage someone's faith by sharing insights He'd given me sparked a fire in me that has burned uncontrollably since. That day, my own dark cloud began to lift. Shortly thereafter, God moved us to our first pastorate, brightening our family's days even more.

I didn't understand for a very long time why we had to go through what we did. So many other seminary families seemed perfectly happy and adjusted well to the life. I asked God then why He ordained that terrible time for me, and I felt Him say, "For her." A plural her.

Second Corinthians 1:3–7 reads,

> *Praise be to the God and Father of our Lord Jesus*
> *Christ, the Father of compassion and the God of all*
> *comfort, who comforts us in all our troubles, so that*
> *we can comfort those in any trouble with the comfort*
> *we ourselves have received from God. For just as*
> *the sufferings of Christ flow over into our lives, so*
> *also through Christ our comfort overflows. If we are*
> *distressed, it is for your comfort and salvation; if we*
> *are comforted, it is for your comfort, which produces*

in you patient endurance of the same sufferings we
suffer. And our hope for you is firm, because we know
that just as you share in our sufferings, so also you
share in our comfort.

Sharing in sufferings; sharing in comfort. How can we comfort if we've never experienced suffering ourselves? If God has never healed us, how do we lead broken people home? God has helped me understand that every single trial I endure serves a twofold purpose: personal refinement and personal ministry. How awesome that He can bring beauty out of our brokenness in the form of a unique way to serve others.

How to Get Out of a Mess

I've shared my dilemma involving a children's ministry and obedience to the command to "make disciples." To me, this is a vital ministry of our church, and whether you agree or disagree, my own conviction is that I must suck up my personal will to see God's will done.

There are also many nonvital activities to be found in the church house, and if you aren't careful, you can find yourself taking on so many of them that you wouldn't have time to do Your Thing even if God caused the sun to stand still in the sky as in the days of Joshua (Josh. 10:13). I define nonvital ministry as anything that, if not done, would not prevent the gospel from going forth. Things like preparing bulletins, mailing birthday cards to members, washing the linens after church functions, cleaning the toilets, and serving on various committees are all great things and seem harmless if taken on one at a time. But together? They spell burnout with a capital B.

If an overloaded schedule filled with activities outside the call is sucking the life out of you, then it's time to evaluate what needs to go. The principles of saying no I've been sharing with you are great if you can apply them to situations you are not yet in. However, many of us are already entangled in a mess we never intended. Here are a few steps to follow when it is obvious it is time to simplify:

Take steps to find a replacement.

Sometimes general pleas are not enough. Ask God to reveal a candidate and ask him or her personally.

Determine whether the ministry is inwardly or outwardly focused.

Be very hesitant to discontinue a true soul-winning ministry. Could Satan be corrupting your desire for sharing God's Word?

Consider the pros and cons.

Which outweighs the other? If continuing the ministry is to the detriment of your family by way of excessively taking you away from them in body and/or spirit, then you can't stop it fast enough.

Pray, pray, pray.

If no one steps up—and you've determined this ministry cannot be let go for the kingdom's sake—ask God to renew personal zeal for it. I've been doing this very thing where the BRT ministry is concerned, and every day I feel little twinges of excitement toward it. That is a miracle in itself.

Exercise the Apollos Principle.

When addressing the believers at Corinth in 1 Corinthians 16:12, Paul said of Apollos, "I strongly urged him to go to you with the brothers. He was *quite unwilling* to go now, but he will go when he has the opportunity."

This verse always makes me cheer. Can you imagine saying no to strong-willed Paul? Apollos made it clear that if he went to Corinth, it would be when he was good and ready. In all respect to Paul, I would have loved to see how he regrouped after that. Just the way he worded his explanation to the Corinthians is enough to make me chuckle. Bravo to Apollos for refusing "strong urgings," no matter how imposing the person making the request. May we always be as bold!

Keeping the Main Thing the Main Thing

It may seem elementary for me to share this final word with you, but time in Scripture study and prayer is the only way you will ever rightly discern your own calling and experience God's sense of favor (or lack of it) over your current routine. The reality of vocational ministry is that we can begin to run our churches like a business rather than a kingdom embassy. This was particularly a problem when we were in college and seminary. It's amazing how we can study *about* God all day and night—and yet our hearts can be far from Him.

Above all things, above all ministries, above all activities, keep God at the center of your yes. Run to Him first when making these hard decisions. I promise, He'll always answer in a way that will glorify Himself while fulfilling you. Check out the Resources in the back of this book for some excellent Bible studies that will help you keep Him the Main Thing while you are doing Your Thing.

Round Table

I heard a great analogy from Bible teacher Nancy Leigh DeMoss just today on the radio. To paraphrase she said, "A woman is either a wall or a door. You can go up against the wall and yet it will stand firm. The door will swing either way." As women in servant leadership, we need to have personal guidelines on when it is appropriate to be unbending or flexible.

The M2M Girls had lots to say about this very thing. Here's what they shared when we talked about the difficulty of setting boundaries:

- "Of the pastors' wives I've known, the one who seemed to have the best handle on things was one who wasn't by nature a people pleaser. She was very loving and an excellent complement to her husband, but she knew where to draw the lines and how to allow others the blessing of serving in their areas of giftedness. Even though this church was also relatively new, her ability to draw effective boundaries kept her from seeming completely worn out. She was a vibrant representative of God, her husband, and her church."—Melinda (layperson)

- "Whenever someone asks you to do something, respond, 'I'll think about it, pray about it, talk to my husband about it, and get back to you by this date.' If they need an immediate response, the answer is no."—Missy @ It's Almost Naptime

- "I take on too much. Sometimes it is because I cannot say no, but mostly I just have unrealistic expectations of myself."— Call Me Mara (name withheld)

- "In our second church we were just beginning to unload the moving van when one of the elders informed me that they had lost the church secretary but had left the job open for me since I would need the money to supplement my husband's income. Do you think we should have turned and run?"—Heather

- "Every good thing isn't a God thing, even ministries in the church. I truly admire the calling God has placed on your lives. Know that some of us don't expect anything from you. Take care of your husband, family, home, and the ministries God has called you to do, and don't worry about what church members are thinking."—Patty @ Girlfriends in God (layperson)

- "Knowing your calling and giftedness is probably the best boundary you can set for yourself and your family."—Missy (layperson)

NOW THAT YOU KNOW:

1. What are your spiritual gifts? How are you exercising them?

2. Are you currently overwhelmed with too many responsibilities in the church? How will you use the Apollos Principle in simplifying your schedule?

3. Are you spending time in God's Word each day? Find a Bible study to keep you in touch with the Main Thing.

4. Laypeople: Do you sense your ministry wives have their fingers in one too many pies? Give them permission to lay something down. Often, they just need to be told it's okay not to work so hard!

Seven

HOW TO RAISE MY PKS
TO KEEP THE FAITH

He [the overseer or pastor] must be one who
manages his own household well, keeping
his children under control with all dignity.
—*1 Timothy 3:4 (NASB)*

If I were to ask one hundred people to complete the sentence, "Preachers' Kids (PKs) are _____," the vast majority would answer, "The worst of all!"

But then, everyone knows PKs (or Vicars' Kids—insert your own term here) got that way by playing with the Deacons' Kids.

However, could there be some truth to the stereotype? According to an informal study conducted in Texas, some 80 percent of preachers' kids are no longer connected to the church as adults.[1] Even if that number is in error, just half of this percentage is a frightening statistic. What in the world is driving the kids of the ministry to abandon the faith?

Another study interestingly notes preachers' kids who no longer attend services do not replace their faith with other religions. They overwhelmingly describe themselves as "believers without a church."[2] Many also admit needing counseling as adults for issues stemming from their years as children of ministers.

I don't know about you, but the idea of impossible-to-meet standards being imposed upon my children, either by me or by the congregation, horrifies me. Something very critical to note is the fact that the number of Baby Busters (those born between the years of 1965 and 1983) serving in the senior pastorate doubled in the two years prior to the 2004 Barna survey.[3] Though I could not find more current numbers, one would reason this trend is continuing. My conclusion? There are many, many young children who are being inducted or born into the ministry along with their young parents. It is imperative as we seek authenticity in ministry that we also consider how this applies to raising our kids in that same freedom.

Living Down to Their Reputation

I despise school fund-raisers. I suppose it is one thing if you have a corporate job and work around people who are interested in buying overpriced wrapping paper or generic candy bars, but this is not our reality. My only contact with the outside world is at church, where dozens of other children from the same school district also attend. On any given Sunday, kids from every grade are waving product leaflets while adults cringe and run the other direction, trying to avoid the obligatory purchase.

I have placed a moratorium on any selling by the McKay kids, but before this was in place my then-six-year-old Sam decided he was going to make an all-out effort during the Candle Sale Extravaganza. I told him if he would do the selling and collecting of money that I would allow it, but that I absolutely would not be involved in the process. He agreed, and I let him go on his merry, candle-selling way.

Big mistake.

There is a senior couple in our congregation whom we love dearly—and thankfully they love us back. Their names are Sam and Lou. Because we have a Little Sam, we lovingly refer to this man as Big Sam. During the Candle Sale Extravaganza, Little Sam asked Big Sam to buy a candle. Several other children had already solicited Big Sam, so he respectfully declined.

For that, Little Sam kicked Big seventy-year-old Sam in the shin.

Big Sam thinks Little Sam hung the moon, so he told on him with a laugh, but obviously Luke and I were completely and utterly mortified. We beat the child every shade of blue, made him apologize, and beat him some more. (I'm exaggerating here, people. Please don't write me letters.) Point being, the kid was punished plenty as we wallowed in our humiliation.

If you have spent any time in ministry, you can most likely add your own story to the one I just told you. However, our kids' infractions may not always be met with the same type of graciousness. What's more, the ministry parent is sometimes the one placing more pressure on the child to adhere to "conduct becoming of a preacher's kid" than those within the congregation. As we consider the subject of parenting

PKs, we have to ask ourselves a major question: How do we find the balance between unreal expectations and healthy accountability?

A Happy Medium

You've probably noticed by now I absolutely love digging on the original Greek and Hebrew words contained in sometimes-hard-to-interpret passages. In considering Scripture related to the qualifications of an overseer (or minister), I found a gem that has shaped my parenting philosophy both in general and especially within the church body.

First Timothy 3:4 says, "He [the overseer or pastor] must be one who manages his own household well, keeping his children under control with all dignity" (NASB). Something about having your child kick an old man in the shin seems to suck the dignity right out of you. Thankfully, after studying on the phrase a bit, I found the true intent. I think you will love it as much as I do.

The word *semnotes* is the Greek word used for "dignity." It means the average or virtue that lies between the extremes of "arrogance that pleases no one" and "endeavoring at all cost of dignity and truth to stand well with the world."[4] Therefore, *semnotes* stands between caring to please nobody and endeavoring at all costs to please everyone. It is the ability to perform well one's duties as a citizen, and in addition to show the dignity that is not from earth but from heaven, thus drawing respect and reverence.[5]

This idea of managing a family with dignity suggests there is a happy medium to be established in what we expect from our children as well as what we allow others to expect from them—one in which the child doesn't make a fool of the parents or the parents one of themselves. I wouldn't be a good preacher's wife if I didn't brag on my husband, so I'll tell you something he did recently that serves as a perfect example.

Recently our church celebrated Pastor Appreciation Day. We belong to a loving, generous fellowship, so this day was one we wholeheartedly enjoyed. During the Sunday evening service, Luke gave a "State of the Union" address in which he thanked the church, let the members know our zeal had not diminished, and communicated how very happy we remain in our ministry. (A little side note—the people to whom you are ministering appreciate knowing when you are happy.)

Then he said something I hadn't anticipated but had me almost giving a "whoop whoop" from my seat: "Thank you for loving my family, especially my children. I know my kids aren't perfect, and I don't expect them to be. What's more is that I really believe you don't demand this of them any more than you do your own children. We appreciate that you let them be who they are without making them feel they have to meet a different standard. This means the world to us, and we just wanted you to know."

My man is *brilliant*.

Whether Luke realized what he'd done or not—and I'm sure he didn't because he doesn't have the Manipulation Gene—he thanked the congregation in advance for grace. While Luke and I strive toward a happy medium in parenting, we have high expectations of our kids and are working diligently to instill the concept of accountability in them. But we also have to balance this with the understanding that the most dangerous thing we can ever do is to hold our kids to a different standard or somehow suggest the "success" of our ministry is directly related to their behavior.

Extreme Parenting

Outside of this happy medium are disturbing extremes. I recently heard a tragic story of a minister whose son's girlfriend had become pregnant. The man stood from the pulpit, son present, and shamed him in front of the congregation while tearfully exclaiming he was no longer fit for ministry because of the evils of his child. More devastating is the fact the congregation took pity on the pastor by joining forces with him to ostracize this kid from the body. What in the world did that poor boy learn? That he was disposable. That he wasn't good enough. That his own father would rather turn him away than risk the judgment of others by showing unconditional love and mercy. I can't imagine how this young man feels about his father now, but more important, I wonder how he feels about his God.

Where is the dignity in that?

On the opposite end of the child-rearing spectrum are ministry families who seek to please no one in either their own behavior or that of their children. It is my experience that any time children are the source of conflict, the tension factor is multiplied exponentially. The mama bear in each of us automatically wants to scoff, "You must be wrong. I know my child, and he would just never do such a thing!" Here's the truth of it: You can never say never where children are concerned. I am in no way saying not to give them the benefit of the doubt or gather all the information before addressing a situation where wrongdoing is accused (a truth I learned firsthand when my oldest got in a fistfight on the front lawn). Our kids need to know we are first and foremost on their side. What I am telling you is that one of the most important things you can do in building a parenting support system between you and your congregation is to invite them into the process of loving and raising your children by being open when others need to discuss matters of behavior.

Unfortunately, I have seen situations where the minister's children were truly misbehaving by doing anything from destroying property to acting like the Devil on the weekend, but church members were too afraid of a backlash from their pastor or, scarier still, their pastor's wife to tell them what was happening. This brewed bitterness toward the PKs from both parents and other kids who perceived them as being outside the reach of the law.

Just this past week my five-year-old daughter, Sydney, was playing with a friend of mine in our congregation. Sydney has three big brothers, so when she gets wound up, the fists start flying. While the two were horsing around, Sydney raised her hand to hit my friend, who quickly said something to the effect of, "No, ma'am. You'd better not hit me!" Sydney puckered up and cried like she was being killed. Of course, my friend was devastated and apologized repeatedly for breaking her heart, but my response was, "She needed humbling!" The child was the most repentant, precious thing the rest of the day. This is just one small example that the greatest gift I can give my young children is the knowledge they are accountable to God and His people in the matter of their behavior. I can't be everywhere the four of them are at every church function, but if they know others are watching them, I can count on them learning the self-control needed to behave appropriately when I am not looking.

Now before you begin thinking I am contradicting myself by saying our kids should earn not only God's favor but man's as well, consider Proverbs 3:3–4:

> *Do not let kindness and truth leave you;*
> *Bind them around your neck,*
> *Write them on the tablet of your heart.*
> *So you will find favor and good repute*
> *In the sight of God and man.* (NASB)

Jesus was also described as having found favor with God and man in Luke 2:52. How ironic that the One who came to proclaim the year of the Lord's favor received it Himself by growing in strength and spirit. Of particular interest to ministry parents is the fact this same phrase was used of young Samuel in 1 Samuel 2:26. While Eli's sons had a poor reputation before the people of Israel, Samuel was approved by God and man. Eli was asked by God in 1 Samuel 2:29, "Why do you honor your sons more than me?" when he refused to deal with their flagrant disobedience.

When people know your family is seeking favor, more often than not you will receive grace. It is the same concept with our heavenly Father. How freely does He bestow grace as we seek favor? Luke 11:13 tells us, "If you then, though you are evil, know how to give good gifts to your children, how much more will your Father in heaven give the Holy Spirit to those who ask him!" Where God is concerned, we can know we are safe in pursuing His delight at all costs because His motivation is our good. Because man's motivations are not always pure, we can fall back to the happy medium in seeking to meet expectations and find balance between not caring at all what is said of us and sacrificing our children on the altar of approval.

Following this general rule of thumb will manifest itself in the lives of your children and the church in this way: When your congregation knows your main goal in the raising of your children is to have them love God and respect His house and His people, then their criticisms will be in love instead of contempt for what you are not doing. I've seen this played out with my very own kids. Luke and I have communicated in many different ways that *we need help* and treasure anyone willing to enter into a Titus relationship with our family. What I've seen is the people who love our family gently guide my kids and then consider their misdeeds dealt with instead of telling me every little time they act up in Children's Church or run through the sanctuary. It's a great arrangement, and our family is stronger for it.

So Far, So Good

The most important result of this happy medium from which we strive to parent came when I asked my own kids, "Do you feel loved by the people in our church?"

Their answer? "Yeah. They kind of spoil us rotten."

I sincerely pray you can characterize the relationship between your family and your congregation with the words *favor* and *grace*. You may have even recognized, as have I, that you sometimes parent in one of the extremes rather than in the happy medium. It is never too late to establish a philosophy within your family and congregation that will create an environment of great love and acceptance for your kids. Ideally, this will also translate into our kids growing into adults who determine to stay connected to the body of Christ rather than feeling a need to run from it.

As in all things, if our children sense joy, stability, contentedness, and peace with God in our lives, they will be much more likely to cope well themselves. My prayer is for the words of my son Elijah to be the reality for your PKs:

"Being the preacher's kid ROCKS!"

Round Table

The M2M Girls had lots of wisdom to share about parenting within ministry:

- "Something I'm sure has helped [my kids] is that my husband has ALWAYS put family first and he expects his staff to do the same. Nothing comes before family events or needs. I truly believe God has blessed that endeavor."—Robin @ Robinznest

- "As a PK, I was asked to serve in different areas more than other kids. This wasn't bad, per se, but I think that Mom tended to volunteer me more than I would have preferred and in areas that I wasn't gifted in. But as the pastor's kid, I should be there every time the door was open!"—Stephanie

- "Because the kids are at the church building ALL the time, they feel very familiar there and aren't always on their best behavior. There was a time when every single Sunday I'd go to pick up one of them and hear a report on her negative behavior. It stung and made me sad, but I was glad they weren't afraid to address it with us."—Cindy @ Still His Girl

- "My fifteen-year-old is definitely expected by others to be a leader among her peers. One day someone asked her a question about the Bible and said, 'You better know the answer, your dad is a pastor.' In her usual quick wit, she snapped back, 'Your dad is a plumber … do you know how to fix a toilet?'"—Kelli @ Ponderings of a Pastor's Wife

- "I think the only times the kids have been angry or disillusioned with the church is when they have caught wind of those people who wanted to bad-mouth their dad."—Susan @ Learning for Lifetime

- "My pastor is very open and vulnerable when talking about his mistakes in parenting. They are really funny things that everyone else can relate to, so he has done a wonderful job connecting with us."—Michele (layperson) @ My Brazilian Life

- "My husband is a student pastor at our church. We have one little girl who is thirteen months old, so we are very new to having a PK. I can tell you I have been praying for her since before we were married because I knew there was no way around her being a PK. I did not know any PKs who were normal, so I was very worried."—Lori @ Welcome to My World

- "There is another area in which we must be careful … our children. I have the opportunity to model faith and godliness in front of them during situations like the one we are going through now. They can either see a momma who exercises self-control and forgiveness when people hurt us, or they can see a loudmouthed woman who gives everybody a piece of her mind. Our children don't need to know everything that happens in the church. It is too much for them to handle. They should be treated as weaker vessels, and we need to be careful not to cause them to stumble."—Kelli @ Ponderings of a Pastor's Wife

Now That You Know:

1. Take your family's pulse often. In what ways do you let your children know they are a priority?

2. Avoid discussing difficult church issues in front of the kids. I wish I had a nickel for every time we've discovered our kids heard something they shouldn't and we've said, "Don't you dare talk about what we just said outside of this house!"

3. Respect the kids' privacy by asking permission to share personal information. I've seen Luke forgo some great sermon illustrations because the child who was the subject changed his mind about letting Dad tell a story about him. No kid wants their every move relayed to the multitudes. Respect the fact they are little people with big feelings.

4. Remind your kids of the blessings of being a PK instead of the curses. Teach them to be grateful for the acts of kindness they will undoubtedly receive.

5. Don't be afraid to be transparent about your own short-comings in parenting. Parishioners appreciate knowing you aren't superhuman.

6. Laypeople: Does your pastor have children? If you want to bless their family, love on the kids. I am encouraged and my heart swells when someone makes the effort to do something special for my little ones.

Eight

ABOUT THE JOYS OF HELLO

I don't know why you say
good-bye, I say hello.
—*The Beatles*

To say Luke and I have moved a lot is a total understatement. I've lost count of our addresses, but my friend Candace told me we take up the entire "M" section of her address book with all the updates over the years. If I ever apply for a government job, she'll be the person I call to fill in the "previous address" section of the application because, seriously, I have no idea.

Most of our relocations have been directly or indirectly related to life in ministry. We've gone away to college, come home, left again to go to seminary, and then followed a series of pulpit ministries across three states. If U-Haul had frequent-driver perks, we'd be upgraded to a leather cockpit and the removal of the sixty-mile-per-hour control on the gas pedal. And for those of you whose churches send you a moving company? Well, good for you. I'm not bitter—really.

The potential for frequent moves is a fact of life for the ministry wife. The Ellison Research group said in a 2005 report,

> *The most common reason for moving from one church to another is a desire to serve in a different type of community or a different region of the country.... Other common reasons for changing jobs are getting promoted to a higher position, such as from an associate pastor at one church to the senior pastor of another church (20%), wanting to pastor a larger church (16%), ... better pay and/or benefits (11%), being fired or asked to leave a church (10%), and switching to a different denomination (9%).*[1]

This same survey also gives the tenure of American senior pastors across all denominations as 7.7 years.[2]

Because some denominations assign pastorates while autonomous churches choose their own, these statistics vary between groups.

No matter how or why you move, the important thing to remember is that you most likely *will*. With that in mind, let's talk about establishing right thinking where this emotional topic is concerned.

In the Beginning, There Was Seminary

I realize not everyone goes to Bible college or seminary, but for those who do, it can be a huge adjustment—especially if you are taking children with you. Luke and I didn't have children when we moved to college, but we graduated with two. We moved home for a short time, had another child, and continued on to seminary, thinking the two experiences would be similar.

We were wrong.

Our first move—from our hometown in Georgia to the hills of Kentucky to attend Clear Creek Baptist Bible College—was one of the most traumatic yet exciting things I have ever done. At the time, my experience with saying good-bye to friends was limited to high school graduation. I lived in the same small town my entire life, so those tearful farewells lasted only until we got in the car and went to the mall together the next day.

The difficult part of moving away from home was leaving the familiar faces and places to start life all over. There would be no more running to my mom's house to chat during my lunch break. The nights of hanging out with our best friends would be a thing of the past. And then there was our beloved church. It was like Noah's flood exploding out of my face our last Sunday there.

But there was another feeling underlying all that sadness: anticipation. Familiar is good, but Luke and I were constantly reminded of ghosts from our pasts—by the ghosts themselves. Any old friends we saw who heard about Luke's call to ministry would laugh their heads off and then proceed to remind us of all the reasons we were completely unqualified.

As hard as moving away was that first time, it was really all about us. Our sadness. Our excitement. Our new life.

And a new life it was. Clear Creek was like C. S. Lewis's Narnia to us—a magical time when all was as it should be. The serene campus was filled with like-minded people all preparing to set the world on fire for Jesus. We made friends quickly with many other married couples, and since none of us had any money we took turns cooking beans and potatoes in one another's homes. Life was good—but it got even better.

After our first son, Sawyer, was born, Luke and I both felt I should leave my campus employment to stay home and raise our child. My days were spent in MOPS groups and playdates while Luke studied and worked for minimum wage in the school's maintenance department to provide for our little family.

I distinctly remember putting Sawyer in the stroller one day and walking the short distance to the student center. Once there I was parched from thirst, so I dug through my purse looking for change to buy a drink. I was one quarter short, and I knew—because we had already rolled every penny of change from the house—that we didn't have one quarter anywhere. With tears streaming down my face I turned away from the soft-drink machine and walked home telling myself (in my best Scarlett O'Hara voice), "As God is my witness, I'll never be hungry [or thirsty] again!"

It turns out that those lean times were the ones that endeared us to that place and to our God. You see, when you are starving, you look for things to fill that grumbling space. When you are unable to satisfy yourself with stuff, then you have plenty of room for a big ol' helping of Him. Those four years passed so quickly, but when Luke graduated, we left with a heart overflowing with Jesus and amazingly without a penny of debt. We moved to Georgia knowing seminary was a likely possibility. We naively thought it would be a continuation of that school enchantment.

It wasn't.

Home Again, For a Minute

Now obviously I'm not trying to discourage seminary families. I know God called us to go there according to His good pleasure. I'm not certain it was book smarts He was after as much as ministry mileage. We had our time in the Happy Bubble. I suppose it was only natural that the Fiery Furnace should follow.

One of the huge differences in our college and seminary experiences was the fact our children were now involved. We had our third son, Sam, while living in Georgia. He was only two months old when we moved. Needless to say, taking him away when he was so brand-new was heart wrenching for me and our extended family. In case you haven't heard, grandmothers detest living long distances from their grandbabies and are typically not happy with the people responsible for the separation. I'm not saying our parents were unsupportive, but I don't think they were quite convinced that Luke's pursuit of more education was necessary and that we weren't exercising cruel and unusual punishment by bringing the children home long enough to get attached and then taking off again. Goodbye this time wasn't bittersweet—it was just bitter.

I've shared these two very different experiences because I want you to know I understand both. I know how it feels to know you are doing exactly what God wants. I also know the feeling of being certain He called you to a place only to soon believe He dropped you off and disappeared. In college, we were flat broke but our needs always seemed to be met—both supernaturally and by the sweat of our brow. In seminary, we were flat broke and, well, *nothing*. No mysterious cards in the mail with money to meet our exact need. No subtraction error in the checkbook that netted an extra few dollars. No available overtime at work. Our debt mounted (after we'd worked so hard to have none), depression abounded, and Satan tried to make me believe Luke made a huge mistake in moving our family. (Notice he tried to make me forget I had been a part of that decision.)

There is deep and abiding value in both realities. We've known people who weren't able to graduate from school and returned home feeling like failures. If you believe in the same sovereign God that I do, then even those things are used for His glory. I didn't understand at the time why seminary was such a deep, dark, depressing time for our family; however, I can look back now and know undeniably that among other things God forged my personal ministry in that fire. Our Happy Bubbles just don't get hot enough to transform a girl into a dramatically shinier version of the original. No matter what your situation where school is concerned—moving there, already there, been there—embrace every moment. The mileage you gain will be much more valuable than any term paper your hubby will ever write (or you will type for him).

Preparing the Kids

If you'll allow me to repeat the obvious, moving with children is exponentially harder than without. I can't tell you a day I don't pray that God will allow us to remain in our current pastorate until all my children have graduated from high school. Seeing as how my youngest just started kindergarten, in my heart of hearts I know this isn't likely to happen.

When we moved here three years ago my oldest son, Sawyer, had just finished third grade. He wasn't taking the idea of a move this time around any better than he did when we moved to North Carolina when he was only four. The child has never liked change, and so when the talk got serious about moving to Alabama, I worried about him most of all. I prayed throughout every day that if God was going to relocate our family, He'd speak to Sawyer about it too.

We began preparing the kids by taking a drive to the new town and showing them the church, the school, and the house where we would live. If at all possible, you should always let your children have a visual of their potential lives so they can daydream about the adventure. I believe wholeheartedly that God uses those images to call the kids to a ministry just as He does us. Call it woman's intuition or the whispers of the Holy Spirit, but the first time I saw the parsonage of the church we now serve, something told me it would be my home.

We didn't push the move on the kids but asked God to help them be curious about what life in Alabama would be like. Sure enough, those questions started coming, and the more we answered, the more excited they seemed. Sawyer was the only holdout. He wasn't talking.

I worried about what we were doing to the poor boy by uprooting him yet again. One night we were saying prayers, and out of the blue he said, "Mom, I've been thinking about Alabama. I think it will be pretty cool if we get to live there." You just have to know this kid, but that statement was a miracle in itself.

As hard as it is to think about, I have to believe God will be faithful in drawing our children anywhere He calls us, even if that means moving us when they are in high school—a horrible thought to me. However, I've heard many testimonies of God's gentle wooing during those hard times, so I'll trust Him to lead us across that bridge if we come to it.

Parsonage or Purchase?

Many churches have moved away from the era of the parsonage due to the simple fact that ministers are choosing to own their homes. Most churches agree to pay all or a portion of the house payment in the form of a housing allowance. The advantage of this arrangement is the minister has the ability to build equity while paying only a portion of his mortgage payment. For the wife, a major advantage is the ability to paint every room in the house fuchsia if her heart so desires. Can we do that in a parsonage? I don't think so.

The downside to home ownership is the hassle of relocation. It is difficult to shop for a home long-distance (if you are moving from another area). Most people have no idea what part of a community they would like to live in until they've had the opportunity to visit the town and research the different schools if kids are involved. Another drawback comes when a minister leaves a congregation. Having to sell a home in order to move can greatly hinder one's freedom to pick up and go. There are also the costs of home maintenance and renovation that can add up quickly, especially if your budget forces you to purchase an older home.

And then, there is the parsonage. (I think I just heard some of you groan.)

Luke and I are exceedingly blessed to have a wonderful home provided by our church. When we needed a playroom for the kids, the men of the church closed in the garage and allowed us to remodel it as a playroom. If something breaks, they take care of the problem immediately. We were able to move straight in without the stress of the purchase process. The house is plenty big and is next door to the church and elementary school. It's simplicity at its finest.

We've also been granted absolute liberty in decorating however we please, which is a huge deal to me. Churches, you do a grave disservice to your minister's wife by not allowing her the freedom to put her personal touch on her home. There is nothing that says, "This isn't your house, so don't get comfortable," like telling a woman she either cannot make any decorative changes to the parsonage or must jump through hoops to get approval. In a previous church, I was told I must submit my color chips to the building and grounds committee to be voted on before I painted anything. Guess whose walls remained stark white?

Of course there are drawbacks to the parsonage life. One peeve of mine is the number of people from our community who will come to our house at ungodly hours for assistance when the church office is closed. A family once woke us at seven on a Saturday to let them into the food pantry, without the first hint of appreciation. (I sound terrible. But these folks were repeat offenders.) Some of my ministry-wife friends don't like the drop-by company they get. That doesn't bother me so much simply because I've learned to not freak out if someone stops in and the house is a wreck. I have four kids and a busy life. If you come see me unannounced, I can't promise what you will find. I live by the motto, "I clean house every other day. Sorry you missed it."

Another disadvantage is the fact no equity is building in a home. A minister must pay taxes on the rental value of the parsonage so technically, it isn't "free." Most accountants counsel heavily against living in a rectory if there is another option, but from my perspective the stress relief of not having a house payment far outweighs the tax relief we would get otherwise. There will be a time when we will own a home again, but we've enjoyed the rest and convenience the parsonage has offered for this season.

Leaving with Head Held High

We've talked about some of the particulars of moving, but perhaps most important is the way in which we say good-bye.

I've already noted the major reasons ministers leave their congregations, but obviously the most difficult way of parting is when conflict is involved. It is hard enough pulling up stakes under good conditions, but add hurt feelings, whirling accusations, flat-out lies, and uncomfortable truths to the mix, and you have yourself a recipe for disaster.

I heard a wise pastor once counsel to never demonize the opposition. So many times when problems arise in the church we automatically assume Satan is using church members as a weapon against our ministry. I'm not saying this isn't sometimes true because the Devil knows his most effective work is done within the church rather than outside it. But I've been around long enough to know that sometimes there can be two very reasonable but differing opinions on one subject, and just because an opinion does not agree with your own does not mean those who oppose you are possessed.

I share this because I've heard and seen some ugly exits from the pulpit. Pastors have punched deacons. They have told off the congregation in a Sunday morning service, leaving visitors in total shock. They have written letters of contempt back to the church, slandering members. They have left in the middle of the night with no explanation or remorse when moral failure was revealed.

All of these are terrible, but wives can do just as much peripheral damage as their husbands. I know of one instance where a pastor's wife became embittered over conflict and so, in a scene worthy of Jerry Springer, maliciously proceeded to share on her way out every confidence women in the church had entrusted to her over the years. (Remember, we do not want to be diabolical!)

Girls, girls, girls. Whatever, and I mean *whatever,* your church has done, you walk out of that place with dignity. Don't make an idiot out of yourself or embarrass your God! Don't act out in the heat of the moment. Don't say anything you'll have to apologize for later. Don't do anything that will hurt innocent people caught in the cross fire. If you want to be sure the unsaved in your community never darken the doors of a church, act like a fool on your way out of one. That should do the trick.

Even though church conflict feels so personal, it really is never about you. You are the smallest part of it. Conducting ourselves in a manner worthy of our calling is our highest obligation. Let the words of 1 Peter 3:16 be your shield: "Keeping a clear conscience, so that those who speak maliciously against your good behavior in Christ may be ashamed of their slander." Against your *good behavior* in Christ. Ain't nobody gonna be ashamed for treating you badly if you're behaving badly.

I'll quit being your mother now.

You're welcome.

The Joys of Hello

A girl could quickly become depressed at the prospect of a life wrought with good-byes. Many ministry wives use this as an excuse to avoid making new friends because it will hurt too badly when it is time to leave.

I will never forget having to say good-bye to my friend Julie when Luke graduated college. Her husband was one of Luke's professors, and our families had become great friends. We both danced around the subject until, finally, moving day was upon us and there was no more avoiding it. We stood in my kitchen until one of us finally said, "Okay, let's do this." We grabbed one another and bawled our eyes out.

Julie and I didn't know each other well until Luke's senior year, and I don't suppose anyone would have blamed either of us for keeping each other at arm's length since it was obvious our time together would be short-lived. There would have been no greater tragedy. Even though our families now live in different states, I still consider her one of my dearest friends and mentors.

Every place you go will hold friendships that will outlast your stay—if you let them. Instead of pining over good-byes, embrace the joy of hellos. I never stop being amazed at the different types of people God blesses me through during different stages of my life. Luke and I are not in a church to do the ministering but to receive it as well. I've received in just great measure, and I know if God calls on us to move forward yet again, there will be an abundance of new faces added to my sisterhood.

Getting to Know You

You know by now that I love the practical. Here are a few things I do that help immensely when I find myself in a new ministry setting:

Study the directory.

Many churches have a directory complete with photos of members. Call me a nerd, but in our last ministry I took one home with me and made notes about who was related to whom, who taught which Sunday school class, etc. It was a great help in learning names and making connections.

Accept invitations.

I mentioned this in the BFF chapter, but I think it is important enough to note again. Though I can never keep up the pace long term, I try my best to attend as many events as possible during the first months of a pastorate. It is impossible to form relationships with people an hour or so a week. We have to be willing to meet with members on their turf in order to be loved and accepted by their families. If you are an introvert, this can be a challenge, but the hard work will pay off in so many different ways in the long run. I've made many new friends over a slice of Dora the Explorer birthday cake.

Go easy.

Restrain yourself from jumping into ministry as soon as you bound through the door. Take it from a girl who often says yes first and asks questions later: It is hard to keep jumping over a highly placed bar. It is much better to take on a few carefully chosen projects slowly than to find yourself in the position of quitting things accepted impulsively.

Prioritize settling your family in your home and community.

This is a follow-up to the previous point. Give yourself plenty of freedom to get your boxes unpacked before getting too busy to stay at home. I always unpack the kids' rooms first and get them completely settled before everything else. This way they have a place to be and can begin feeling settled while you work in the other areas.

Take the time to get to know your new town. Is there a movie theater, a zoo, an ice cream parlor that you can see becoming a family favorite? Take the time necessary to explore before overobligating yourself to other activities.

Expect comparisons to the last minister's wife.

I have discovered people fall into two camps where the last wife was concerned: She was either fabulous because of all her Dorcas-like works or detested because she "didn't do a thing around the church" or was a gossip.

Though both circumstances can be awkward, don't be offended either way. Who knows the motivation of people who share these things with us? Do they expect us to do all the stuff the last girl did? Maybe. Are we being true to ourselves by trying to be like her? Absolutely not. When someone shares all the terrible things about the last pastor's wife, I've found it's just a strange way of trying to bond. Don't get caught up in the tales. If the last exit was a bad one, chances are the memories of all the poor woman did are exaggerated. Just give it the Smiley Nod and move on.

Round Table

I'm not the only one with a few tips on managing a move. These M2M Girls are brilliant!

- "When you say good-bye, try to get together with those people who are closest to you. Tell them how they've positively impacted your ministry in that place. If it's a 'bad good-bye,' then ask God to help you deal with any pain or bitterness that has been caused. If you don't forgive the experience and the people, you'll carry it to your next appointment."—Susan @ Learning for Lifetime

- "My pastor friend once told me, 'Beware of the first ten people you meet.' You know, the ones that are dying to meet you first so they can give you the scoop on how things are or should be, in their eyes."—Annie (layperson) @ Annie's Eyes

- "A good thing to remember when leaving one place of ministry is not to leave before you are gone. That just means once you know you are moving, sometimes it is hard to stay and finish strong."—Jeannette @ Abound in Hope

- "Before moving, we always throw a going-away party for each of our children, and I try to find something to give them that will last. I once had all their friends sign a pillowcase with permanent markers. They still use it! I also had my son's friends sign his guitar. He has it hanging in his room now."—Sara @ Sara's Blog

- "I already love our new pastor and his wife, but I also desperately miss the previous pastor's family. The PW was someone I could always rely on to tell the hard truth, and she's irreplaceable. They've distanced themselves, and I think it was the right thing to do, but it still makes me kind of sad."—Bethany (layperson) @ Beyond This Moment

- "Our second youth pastorate was really hard because the last YP and his wife were really loved. We both felt compared to them a lot. I feel like there was always somewhat of a shadow there that we would never be able to get out from under, no matter what we did. That is a really difficult place to be."—Jennifer @ Perspective from the Parsonage

- "We've been offered the 'rich and famous' contract a few times, but the longer we stay where we are, the more we see the long-term impact of life-on-life ministry. It makes me so sad when I see other pastors' families having to move every few years."—Michelle @ Dawning Light

Now That You Know:

1. What is your attitude toward ministry moves? Ask God to give you the strength to be positive if you are transplanted.

2. Do you tell your husband when you are grieving a move? Keep lines of communication open so that silent sadness doesn't turn to bitterness.

3. For those of you who live in a parsonage, do you feel at home? If not, have a heart-to-heart with the church leadership and let them know the importance of putting your touch on your living space.

4. Read the account of Paul saying good-bye to the Ephesian elders in Acts 20:13–38. What strikes you about the way in which the elders and Paul parted ways?

5. Laypeople: Nothing, and I do mean *nothing*, will thrill your new ministry wife more than a well-timed meal when she is settling into her home. If your minister is moving into a parsonage or rectory, stock the refrigerator with a few snacks and necessities so an immediate trip to the grocery store isn't needed. Again, give the minister's wife liberty in decorating the home. A few gallons of paint when the family moves will cost far less than the damage done to her heart if she isn't allowed to make the house her home.

Nine

THE GREATEST GIFT IS LOVE

Above all, love each other deeply, because
love covers over a multitude of sins.
—*1 Peter 4:8*

As I near the end of this book, I can't help but be sentimental toward the congregation we now serve that has lovingly embraced my family—and specifically me as their pastor's wife.

I can honestly say Luke and I are privileged to be part of one of the most loving bodies of people we've ever known. I'm certain you have your own criteria where judging the affections of your parishioners is concerned. I know our people love us by the genuine interest they take in the day-to-day life of my family. We have church members who come to watch my kids play ball. Others share from the bounty of their gardens. Yet more send encouraging cards in the mail and remember our special days. Each year the church makes a huge deal out of Pastor Appreciation Month. And of course there are the quiet handshakes with a folded bit of money inside that let us know this flock wants to provide for our needs in every way.

I know all of the things I just mentioned touch Luke, but the most encouraging thing for him in church life is for someone's eyes to light up—for them to finally "get it." Get they have the power of the Holy Spirit to overcome the Evil One. Get that God loves them with breadth, depth, and width that surpasses knowledge. Get that He means for them to serve the body. Get that it's a joy to dwell in the house of the living God and to commune with His people. Zeal for the house is the greatest gift anyone can give either of us, so when those times come and a fresh face steps us and says, "God has been showing me it's time for me to get busy"—and then he or she actually plugs in? Oh my, how the rejoicing goes on in our family!

As Luke's wife I often tell people, "When you've blessed Luke, you've blessed me. When you've loved Luke, you've loved me. When you've encouraged Luke, you've encouraged me." And I mean that from the depths of my heart. Since I believe I am placed here to do what I can to uphold this man's ministry, it is only natural that my heart would want to explode when I see the sheep he loves so deeply love him back.

Luke and I have served many people in different locations and capacities. Even though we felt loved by each group, the way they expressed their affection varied tremendously. Every church has its own unique personality, and we've found that some are easier to be accepted into than others. It's not always that they don't *like* you. They just don't love you. Love takes time. It takes interest. It takes more than one hour per week.

Inspiring Loyalty

I've always been touched and inspired by the love relationship the apostle Paul formed with his churches. Even when he found it necessary to issue a rebuke, it was from the motivation of godly jealousy for the individuals who were his very heart and soul. Loyalty is reciprocal; you have to give it to get it. Paul proved time and time again that he was willing to suffer any hardship for the benefit of those God had entrusted to his care. After a while, the Corinthians finally got it (2 Cor. 7:8–11).

The Book on Leadership by John MacArthur is one of my all-time favorites on the subject. Dr. MacArthur speaks about the necessity of loyalty in a great pastor. He says, "Leadership hinges on trust, and trust is cultivated by loyalty. Where trust is born and respect is maintained, sacrificial, devoted service is rendered. Another way to say this is that our hearts have to be in our people, and our people have to be in our hearts."[1]

Luke and I have never expected to walk into a church and be automatically loved. Loyalty must be earned, and the minister and his family must humble themselves by working to build that trust, which can only come over time.

I have to take a minute to brag on Luke—again. One of the highest compliments people in our community give him is the fact that he is willing to do hard work with his hands. Luke has the work ethic of a mule, was a construction worker prior to ministry, and just happens to be very handy with tools. Not long after we moved to our current pastorate, a terrible storm hit our community and blew down many trees on the property of one of our widows. Luke showed up on the workday, chain saw in hand, and worked shoulder to shoulder with the men of our church until the last bits of brush were cleared away. That one act did more to build trust between these men and him than if he'd visited each of their homes twenty times. People need to be shown, not just told, that you are invested in their welfare.

Don't Give Up

John MacArthur goes on to say about the Corinthian church, "Lots of pastors would have been tempted to give up on such a troublesome church. Not Paul. He was the epitome of a faithful leader."[2]

Girls, I'm so afraid we give up too easily and that as soon as we are no longer feeling the love, we are ready to cut and run. The honeymoon period in a church can be likened to that of a marriage. Typically people are trying harder to be nice to you in the beginning. They are serving in greater capacity. They are excited about the new pastor's vision for the church. A wise man once told us that it takes two years to be in a position relationally to really begin the work of a pastor. The trouble is that at the end of those two years, zeal is diminished, the honeymoon is over, and people begin to lower their masks just a bit and show who they really are. And I'm not just talking laypeople here—pastors and their families can be just as guilty.

The same mentality that has blighted the marriage institution has also infiltrated the church. When the roses have faded and the fireworks have burned out, our "all about me" society tells us it is time to move on to the next parade.

If there was ever a man who had reason to give up on a church, it was Paul. The man had poured years of blood, sweat, and tears into this group of people only for his authority and motivation to be questioned. No doubt Paul asked himself how these people could possibly treat him this way. How could they not know his heart toward them? Paul could have shaken the dust off and written this congregation off as a lost cause, but instead he did the hard thing by fighting it through with them. In the end, there was repentance and a deeper bond developed because the relationship had been tested by fire.

What am I saying? Don't expect effective ministry always to be sappy sweet. We aren't supposed to skip through wildflower fields hand in hand with our people, though it is nice when we are allowed to experience times of love and peace. Sometimes we have to be willing to get in the wrestling ring and muscle our way to an understanding. Both sides may walk away with a limp, but that's a good thing. It's during those times we learn to hold up one another. That is true relational ministry.

Displays of Affection

In writing this chapter I began wondering if our congregation was as sure of my love for them as I am of theirs for me. What types of things do we look for from one another as evidence of our devotion? In an attempt to answer this question, I asked the ministry wives who read my blog to share what things the congregation did to demonstrate their love toward their family. Likewise, I asked laypeople to share the same thing about their pastor and his wife. After analyzing all the responses, allow me to present (in no particular order because that, girls, involves icky math) a Top Ten List of both.

Top Ten Ways a Layperson Knows Her Minister and Minister's Wife Love Her

1. They follow up on my requests for prayer and concerns of my heart.

2. They are open, authentic, and not afraid to share their struggles.

3. They love and socialize with every person equally.

4. They take time to serve through acts of kindness.

5. I know I can call on them with any problem and they will be there for me.

6. They give unconditional love even when I've failed.

7. My pastor's wife always welcomes me with a hug.

8. They personally minister to me in my distress.

9. They take the time to learn my name.

10. They take a genuine interest in my life. My pastor's wife sends personal notes of prayer and encouragement.

Top Ten Ways a Pastor and His Wife Know Their Congregation Loves Them

1. They serve the body with zeal and are faithful to the church.

2. They offer words and notes of encouragement and earnestly pray for us.

3. They take an active interest in our family's life and spend time with us outside of the church.

4. They support the pastor against naysayers in the church.

5. They dote on our children, especially if we live far from family.

6. They invite us into their homes or bring a meal when they sense one is needed.

7. They meet our physical needs financially—often at just the right time.

8. They don't harbor unrealistic expectations from us.

9. They encourage time away for us to be refreshed.

10. They surprise us with random acts of kindness to let us know we are in their hearts and prayers.

I don't know about you, but these lists were extremely eye-opening for me. One of the pastors' wives who read all of the survey responses said, "After reading the comments from the laypeople, I will be doing some things differently. Thanks!" I second that motion. To paraphrase Dr. Gary Chapman's wonderful book *The Five Love Languages,* we can't speak one another's Love Languages if we don't know the words. Seeing in black and white the concrete ways I can bless our congregation gives me fresh motivation to act in ways I know will be received as confirmation of my affection for them.

A Message to the Masses

It has been my heart's desire during the writing of this book for it to be a tool not only for ministry wives but also for the congregations they serve. I am convinced that if we take the time to understand one another, ministry tenure would increase and conflict would decrease.

Laypeople, the main thing that ministry wives want you to know is that their family loves you. Philippians 1:8 says, "God can testify how [we] long for all of you with the affection of Christ Jesus." When God called us out to leave what was comfortable, we were able to obey because He equipped us with a supernatural affection for you—His cherished people.

We are going to mess up. We are going to fail you. We are going to turn right when we should have turned left. I am speaking for my own family, and I will presume to speak for others, when I say that it is rarely with ill intention or impure motive that we err. Luke and I take very seriously the grave responsibility we have of leading God's flock, and we bathe our actions and decision making in prayer.

However, that doesn't make us immune to mistakes. Will you be forgiving? We may be imperfect, but we still desperately want to serve God by serving you. Will you let us?

In our defense, there are often two legitimate sides of an issue—and yet we are forced to choose one. If our choice falls on the opposite side of your own opinion, will you love us anyway? Can we agree to disagree and move on side by side even if we don't feel like holding hands at the moment? When we can operate beyond our own desires and seek God's agenda for our lives and churches, everyone wins. Above all, may God and His kingdom reign.

A Final Exhortation

Girls, it is my prayer that above all things you will love your God, support your pastor husband, and be continuously thrilled over the life and ministry you've graciously been called to live. Can it be hard? Yes—often excruciatingly so. But you will also find yourself experiencing joy in the most unexpected ways and places, and when you do, you'll know that no one but God could have dreamed such a thing.

Don't you dare attempt to live this life alone, or Satan will have you for lunch in no time flat. Be strong, let the Word of God abide in you, overcome the Evil One because greater is He that is in you than he that is in the world. Dear ones, how I pray for you that your hearts will not fail. Remember, there is no more excuse for isolation. God is never more than a prayer away and should always be the first place you run. If you are in an overwhelming place, by all means reach out to a trustworthy friend. If you do not have someone in whom you can confide—or even if you do—you are never farther than an Internet connection away from hundreds of women who understand.

Come visit with us. We are waiting.

Appendix A

FOR PASTORS ONLY:
CAN WE TALK?

Luke and I are friends with a couple from church named Clay and Tammy, who have become very dear to us. We sometimes eat Sunday lunch together at a local buffet. This restaurant has a carved-meat counter where the same man has worked as long as we can remember. He greets every single woman with, "Hello there, pretty thang! How are you doing today, foxy mama?" and if he weren't so portly and innocent (and if he didn't cook such a great steak), I might be offended. As it is, we laugh it off and go our way.

Our children and husbands didn't know this man always made such comments, and one particular Sunday, Clay and Tammy's daughter ran back to tell her dad that the man at the meat counter had been flirting with her mother. Tammy wasn't back to the table yet, and Clay just laughed like it didn't affect him in the least. In fact, Tammy has often commented that Clay doesn't have a jealous bone in his body. Ultimately that can be a good thing, but every woman wants to know that her husband gets a little envious if someone makes goo-goo eyes at her. Being the friend that I am, I decided to point that out.

I said, "Clay, would you like to score some major points with your wife? When she gets back over here, you pitch a fit and act like it really bothers you that some man spoke inappropriately to her. You watch, she will *love* it."

He did it.

And she loved it.

I'm not sure if she knows I gave him the hint, but even if she does, I hope it still means something to her that he cared enough to go along.

Here Are Your Hints

Okay, guys. It is with great respect and humility that I address you on behalf of your darling wives. I've just given her a book full of advice on how to encourage you. Will you hear a few things you can do for her in return?

Give her permission to be nothing but your wife and the mother of your children (if applicable).

Another handclap to Luke for always reaffirming, "Lisa, I don't expect you to do one thing at the church you don't want to do. Being my wife and the mother of our kids is enough to keep you as busy as you need to be." On the flip side, I've met many women who resent their husband's assumption that she is meant to be his personal assistant who takes care of all his administrative duties with little or no gratitude. The less you expect from her, the more you will get.

Also, affirm her gifts. Each of your wives is talented in her own way. Encourage her if she feels led to step into a ministry. Cheer her on as she has cheered you!

Appreciate her efforts.

I recently talked with a pastor's wife who truly made sure her husband never had to lift a finger administratively in his position. She did everything from making all the arrangements for church functions to ordering supplies for the office. Do you know what she told me? "It isn't that I don't enjoy doing all that. It's just that my husband has never once said thank you. He's never acknowledged what he would do if I didn't take care of all his details. Maybe I sound like a baby, but I just want him to appreciate me."

Go out of your way to notice the way your wife serves you and the body. Want to know how to bless her? Keep up the home front for a few hours when she needs alone time. You'll put a fresh bounce in her step—I promise!

Set boundaries.

Your wife is hurt when you come home but can't leave the church behind. As difficult as it can be, work to compartmentalize your life to some degree so you can enjoy the rest and refreshment she wants to give you. When you go home—*be* home!

Protect her.

Again, I humbly respect how difficult it is to shoulder problems of the church alone. I know because I am married to a man just like you. One thing Luke has done for me is to protect me from information that will be hurtful to me or cause me to view someone in a negative light. He doesn't share details of counseling sessions or even tell me if someone has been petty toward him. Obviously, I find it out sometimes on my own and there are situations that require my involvement, but overall I think he desires to shield me from anything negative he can. Though I don't expect it, I love him for it. I know your wife will too.

Make certain your church knows your wife and children are your priority.

This may seem like a given, but there are many, many pastors who have no system of rating what requires them to be absent from their families. Luke made it clear from day one of our current ministry that if he had to choose between some church activity or denominational meeting and our kids' ball games, then the games would win every time. Again, there have been exceptions, but they are very rare. I have no doubt that Luke treasures us, so that makes the times he has to be away much more bearable than if he were consistently gone for things that rate as insignificant or things that should be easily taken care of during the workday. With that said, publish office hours when you are available for counseling, etc., and do your best to stick to them. People don't wait until the doctor's office is closed to schedule a visit. There's nothing wrong with expecting them to make an appointment during your office hours as well.

This is a short list to get you thinking about ways to bless your darling wife. She wants to serve you well or she wouldn't have picked up this book. Return the favor, dear minister.

You'll score some major points with her.

You're welcome.

Appendix B

BLOGGING

Throughout this book, I have shared repeatedly that much of the survey information was derived from my personal blog, The Preacher's Wife (www.APreachersWife.com). If you've been asking, "What in the world is a blog?" then here is a simplified answer according to the Web site Wikipedia:

> *A blog (a contraction of the term "weblog") is a type of website, usually maintained by an individual with regular entries of commentary, descriptions of events, or other material such as graphics or video. Entries are commonly displayed in reverse-chronological order. "Blog" can also be used as a verb, meaning to maintain or add content to a blog. Many blogs provide commentary or news on a particular subject; others function as more personal online diaries. A typical blog combines text, images, and links to other*

blogs, Web pages, and other media related to its
topic. The ability for readers to leave comments in
an interactive format is an important part of many
blogs.[1]

Now, that's the technical definition. Blogs can be either much more technical or much simpler than this condensed description. There are many types of blogs that I won't attempt to define here. For our purposes, I will focus on the "personal journal" aspect of blogging.

My Bloggy Story

One of my favorite ministries is Living Proof, which belongs to Bible teacher Beth Moore. (Maybe you've heard of her?) In February of 2007, I visited her Web site, and the words "LPM Blog—New!" in the lower right-hand corner caught my eye.

The only time I'd heard of a blog was during the previous presidential election. News correspondents reported that the personal views expressed by bloggers were actually powerful enough to sway voting. With this in mind, my visual was limited to left- and right-wing pundits hacking away at a keyboard, hoping to say just the thing to convince someone to elect their candidate. Unless Beth had turned activist, I had no idea why her darlin' self had a blog. I couldn't click the link fast enough.

What I found was no political commentary but rather a series of personal entries from Beth and her daughter Amanda, describing anything from the ministry's Christmas party to Beth's work on her next Bible study. Under each entry was a section of comments where readers were allowed to leave feedback. I discovered that if the commenters also had a blog, I could click on their names and be taken to their personal site. I was immediately fascinated by the possibilities. Within two hours, I had created my own blog and unwittingly entered a community that would change my life in more ways than I could imagine.

Finding Your Niche

When I first began carving out my own little place in the blogosphere, I was concerned about the content of the sites I would visit and the types of people who would visit mine. That issue was quickly laid to rest when I discovered how to connect with women who blogged with my same purpose—meeting friends while magnifying Christ.

There are many genres within the blog community—much as with literature. The particular group I am part of is sometimes referred to as Mommy Blogs. Even though my writing is not limited to my parenting adventure, it certainly doesn't exclude it either. Mommy Blogs are called such more for their demographic than content.

Within each genre are subgroups of blogs called webrings. This is where you will find blogs that target specific interests. My favorite webring is www.ChristianWomenOnline.net, hosted by Christian Women Online, and features over two thousand blogs from women of faith. I also host a webring on my blog specifically for ministry wives. There are many more rings out there, but I think these few thousand will keep you busy for a while.

In Real Life

These days with the popularity of blogging as well as sites like eHarmony and Match.com, the stigma attached to meeting people online for the purpose of friendship and even marriage has lessened. However, years ago when the Internet was first exploding, I thought people who met their mates through personals and computers were just plain weird.

If you would have told me then that I would jump at the opportunity to meet someone in person that I'd "talked" with online, I'd have laughed the same as if you'd said I would one day stop getting spiral perms.

The times, they are changin'.

The reality is, I've now met and become real-life friends with many girls (no boys, never boys!) who were first online acquaintances. Bloggers call these meetings a MIRL—or Meet in Real Life. My first MIRL came when someone whose blog I frequented noticed I also lived in a small town in Alabama. After an email exchange, we quickly figured out we lived only forty-five minutes from each other. We had lunch soon afterward, and the rest is history. Our friendship has now transcended the blog world—as all real friendships should.

A Word of Caution

I am a huge advocate of blogs and the outlet they can offer a minister's wife to share her heart with other women who understand the intricacies of her life. For many obvious reasons it is very difficult for a woman in this position to share her entire heart where her church is concerned—especially if conflict is part of it. Many bloggers, myself included, consider the hobby cheap therapy. I'm only half-joking. There have been many women who have approached me privately by email for wise counsel in the midst of trying times both personally and within the church. Because I don't know them or the church situation, they feel free to divulge the details they've been forced to hold back. It's a release for them and a ministry opportunity for me. On the flip side, I've also dumped on a long-distance friend who just happens to work in the pastoral care office of a large church. It's such a relief to be able to tell it all to someone without repercussions.

I do feel the need to caution you against overdivulging sensitive details on your public postings. I have cringed while reading the blogs of some ministry wives, knowing there would likely be repercussions within the church body when the content was shared on Sister Susie's Hotline. If you think your church members don't know you have a Web site, think again! Be wise when writing and always consider whether your take on a situation could be hurtful, misconstrued, or just flat-out inappropriate to share in the blog format. Bottom line, if you wouldn't want your husband reading it from the pulpit, then don't publish!

The danger in blogging is the temptation to withdraw from face-to-face relationships and immerse oneself in a virtual reality with no real personal obligation. In a busy world that is already disconnected, the convenience-store mentality of friendship only serves to heighten isolation. Blogging should never be used as a replacement for flesh-and-blood relationships but rather as a wonderful addition to them. If you are as blessed as I've been, it can also be a tool for meeting new friends whose paths may never have crossed your own otherwise.

Want to Try Blogging?

There are many different free blogging platforms, but two stand out as the most popular and user-friendly: Blogger (www.blogger.com) and WordPress (www.wordpress.com).

Both of these services have pros and cons, but in the event you decide to have a blog designer create a customized template to further define your online personality, you will want to be on Blogger. There are two reasons I say this: (1) Most blog designers are more familiar with this format, and (2) you must pay a yearly fee for WordPress if you use a custom template versus one of the templates they provide. Another word of advice? Don't put any money into blogging until you've determined it is something you plan to do long term.

Either service you choose offers easy-to-follow instructions for establishing your own blog. Simply follow their instructions to get started.

Helpful Hints

There are a few things to keep in mind when beginning a blog:

1. Choose a name that identifies your online personality. I chose The Preacher's Wife because many people in my small town call me that instead of my name.

2. Attempt uniformity with the Web URL and email address you create. For example, my blog name is The Preacher's Wife, my Web URL is www.APreachersWife.com, and my email is

thepreacherswife1@gmail.com. Establishing your identity in this way will keep your blog audience from becoming confused about who you are when communicating with you.

3. To protect your privacy, create a generic email address that is only attached to your blog. Use Yahoo!, Gmail, Hotmail, etc.

4. Expanding on the idea of privacy, determine ahead of time how much information about yourself you are willing to divulge. Because I write regularly for publication, I give my first and last name, but many women choose not to do this. I do not tell my children's names nor do I advertise the town in which we live. Some women are very careful not to publish pictures of their children, while others have them in practically every post. Again, this is a matter of personal preference, but you should decide what your limits will be and stick to them.

5. Blogging can be very time-consuming. Set a timer so you don't allow a few minutes to turn into a few hours. Reward completed housework with a few minutes to write a new post. And never let time on the computer replace your time in the Word!

6. If you start a blog, you are obligated to tell me first! I joke with my hometown girlfriends that all blog activity must be reported to me immediately. By all means, if you jump in,

come say hello so I can return the blessing! Hope to see you soon.

Appendix C

RESOURCES

Here you will find a few resources that are helpful to me when I need encouragement in my role as a ministry wife. I hope you will find them encouraging too!

Online

Anita Renfroe: Anita is a Christian comedienne, author, and pastor's wife who makes me laugh my head off. Need a smile? Check her out! (www.AnitaRenfroe.com)

Christian Coalition Against Domestic Abuse: Florida-based organization with a special understanding of and ministry to women abused by their pastor husbands. I pray none of you need this link but, if you do, *you will find help*. (www.CCADA.org)

Christian Women Online—The Preacher's Wife Column (www.ChristianWomenOnline.net/LisaMcKay.html)

Global Pastors' Wives Network (www.GPWN.org)

Just Between Us—Jill Briscoe (www.JustBetweenUs.org)

Lois Evans' Pastor's Wives Ministry (www.LoisEvans.org)

Married to the Ministry Blogroll:
> A large listing of ministry wives serving in positions ranging from the senior pastorate to missionaries to evangelists. You are sure to find community here! (www.APreachersWife.com/index.php/2008/04/16/Married-to-the-Ministry-Blogroll/)

The Parsonage: Absolutely full of articles and resources for the ministry family. Perhaps my favorite site in this list! (www.Parsonage.org)

The Preacher's Wife (www.APreachersWife.com)

Books (I love every single book on this list!)

Briscoe, Jill. *Renewal on the Run*. Birmingham, AL: New Hope, 2005.

Cloud, Henry, Dr., and Dr. John Townsend. *Boundaries*. Grand Rapids, MI: Zondervan, 1992.

Dobson, Lorna. *I'm More than the Pastor's Wife*. Grand Rapids, MI: Zondervan, 1995.

George, Denise. *What Women Wish Pastors Knew.* Grand Rapids, MI: Zondervan, 2007.

Langberg, Diane. *Counsel for Pastors' Wives.* Grand Rapids, MI: Zondervan, 1988.

London. H.B., and Neil B. Wiseman. *Married to a Pastor.* Ventura, CA: Regal, 1999.

MacArthur, John. *The Book on Leadership.* Nashville: Nelson, 2004.

Pannell, Nancy. *Being a Minister's Wife and Being Yourself.* Nashville: B&H Publishing Group, 1993

Patterson, Dorothy. *Handbook for Minister's Wives.* Nashville: B&H Publishing Group, 2002.

Notes

Chapter Two

1. Spiros Zodhiates, *The Hebrew-Greek Key Word Study Bible* (Chattanooga, TN: AMG Publishers, 1984), 1728.
2. *The Blue Letter Bible,* s.v. "Strong's G3525—*nēphō*," http://www.blueletterbible.org/lang/lexicon/lexicon.cfm?Strongs=G3525&t=KJV (accessed November 20, 2008).
3. Muriel L. Whetstone Sims, "Groomed to Be a First Lady," *On the Forefront,* http://www.loisevans.org/site/c.nkI2KhMWItF/b.2233049/k.2345/Reading_Rm__Pg7__LE_groomedToBe.htm (accessed August 24, 2008).
4. Zodhiates, *The Hebrew-Greek Key Word Study Bible,* 1728.
5. Ibid., 1721.
6. Ibid., 1678.

Chapter Three

1. "Pastors, Wives Urged to Exemplify Marriage," *The Florida Baptist Witness,* June 28, 2007, http://www.floridabaptistwitness.com/7525.article (accessed September 17, 2009).
2. Ibid.

3. Zodhiates, *The Hebrew-Greek Key Word Study Bible*, 1712.

4. Christian Coalition Against Domestic Abuse, "Statistics," http://ccada.org/stats.aspx (accessed September 17, 2009).

5. John Piper, *What's the Difference? Manhood and Womanhood Defined According to the Bible* (Wheaton, IL: Crossway Books, 1990), 22.

6. The Barna Group, "Pastors Paid Better, But Attendance Unchanged," March 29, 2001, http://www.barna.org/barna-update/article/5-barna-update/39-pastors-paid-better-but-attendance-unchanged (accessed September 15, 2009).

7. Dave Ramsey, "Two for the Money," *Focus on the Family,* April 2007, www2.focusonthefamily.com/focusmagazine/christianliving/A000000826.cfm (accessed September 15, 2009).

Chapter Four

1. Diane Langberg, *Counsel for Pastors' Wives* (Grand Rapids, MI: Zondervan, 1988), 14.

2. *The American Heritage Dictionary of the English Language,* 4th ed., s.v. "Proactive."

3. John MacArthur, *The Book on Leadership* (Nashville: Nelson, 2004), 26–27.

4. Dorothy Patterson, *Handbook for Ministers' Wives* (Nashville: B&H Publishing Group, 2002), 214.

Chapter Five

1. Alexander Balmain Bruce, *The Training of the Twelve* (New York: Doubleday, 1963), 29–30.

2. *NASB Study Bible* notes: 1 Sam. 20:3 (Grand Rapids, MI: Zondervan, 1999), 375.

Chapter Six

1. Beth Moore, *Feathers from My Nest* (Nashville: B&H Publishing Group), 139.

Chapter Seven

1. John Hall, "Most Preachers' Kids Reject Church, Informal Survey Reveals," *The Baptist Standard*, March 19, 2004, http://www.baptiststandard.com/index.php?option=com_content&task=view&id=1688&Itemid=1322 (accessed August 12, 2007).

2. Hijme Stoffels, "Preachers' Kids Are the Worst," Association for the Sociology of Religion, San Francisco, CA (August 14, 2004), http://hirr.hartsem.edu/sociology/articles/stoffels.pdf, 8.

3. The Barna Group, "A New Generation of Pastors Places Its Stamp on Ministry," February 17, 2004, http://www.barna.org/barna-update/article/5-barna-update/135-a-new-generation-of-pastors-places-its-stamp-on-ministry (accessed September 18, 2009).

4. Zodhiates, *The Hebrew-Greek Key Word Study Bible*, 1728.

5. Ibid.

Chapter Eight

1. Ellison Research, "Study Shows Why Protestant Clergy Change Jobs," September 7, 2005, http://www.ellisonresearch.com/ERPS%20II/release_18_jobs.htm (accessed September 18, 2009).

2. Ibid.

Chapter Nine

1. MacArthur. *The Book on Leadership*, 70.

2. Ibid., 71

Appendix B

1. Wikipedia contributors, "Blog," *Wikipedia, The Free Encyclopedia,* http://en.wikipedia.org/wiki/Blog (accessed July 21, 2008).